ROVER 800 SERIES

The Complete Story

First published in 2016 by
The Crowood Press Ltd
Ramsbury, Marlborough
Wiltshire SN8 2HR

www.crowood.com

British Library Cataloguing-in-Publication Data
A catalogue record for this book is available from the British Library.

ISBN 978 1 78500 224 3

Typeset by Jean Cussons Typesetting, Diss, Norfolk

Printed and bound in Malaysia by Times Offset (M) Sdn Bhd

CONTENTS

INTRODUCTION AND ACKNOWLEDGEMENTS

The Rover 800 was more of a milestone in the car industry than most people realize. It was the largest and most comprehensive joint project ever undertaken by two companies that were not only independent but also geographically and culturally separated by a vast divide. That it was any kind of success is certainly a tribute to the dedication of the engineers at Rover in Britain and at Honda in Japan who worked on it.

Was it a success? On Rover's side, it provided them with a large car that they badly needed and could not afford to design and manufacture on their own. It taught them new manufacturing disciplines and edged them towards the quality that had been lost during the British Leyland years of the 1970s. That it never sold in quite the anticipated numbers was mostly not the car's fault – although the bad reputation that British Leyland had attracted still lingered to some extent and must have deterred many buyers. On Honda's side, it provided them with their first large car and gave them valuable experience of both the European and American large-car markets. The Japanese company has never looked back.

The 800 Series has taken a long time to become an enthusiast's car, but I was delighted to discover – just as this book was in the final stages of preparation – that it was to have its own formal club. The Rover 800 Owners' Club was officially launched at the NEC Classic Motor Show in November 2015, and I wish it every success.

In putting this book together, I drew on the vast collection of material in my own archive, amassed since the 800 was new in 1986. I can still remember trying out an 825i demonstrator over the summer of that year, one of the Cxxx AAC registered cars, and being encouraged to see how fast it would go on the M4 motorway. I needed no encouragement, and a nervous salesman suggested that we should keep a sharp look out for police cars when the speedo nudged 115mph. So I backed off. I didn't buy the car, either, and will admit now that I was never a fan of the early 800. Once the Fastback became available, though, and then the facelifted cars in 1991, my view changed to one of keen interest.

I was pleased to be able to draw to a limited extent on the archives of the British Motor Museum at Gaydon (formerly British Motor Industry Heritage Trust), although surviving records of Rover 800 production are far from complete. I hope that more hard information comes to light in the future. I also drew on the collections and recollections of many others, most of whom may well not even remember passing on vital information all those years ago. Special thanks, though, go to the following: Richard Bryant, long-term friend and long-term enthusiast for Rover cars of all ages (and an 800 Sterling KV6 owner himself); Paddy Carpenter of the Police Vehicle Enthusiasts' Club; Sally Eastwood, whose recollection of the end of the US Sterling operation is recorded in Chapter 5; Ian Elliott, formerly involved with PR and marketing at Austin Rover; Tanya Field, who kindly provided her 1991 820 Turbo for photography (she was lucky I gave it back); David Morgan, researcher and great enthusiast for Austin Rover cars; and Ron and Pam Winchester, for the loan of their Japanese-spec Coupé while I was in New Zealand.

James Taylor
Oxfordshire
November 2015

FOREWORD

by John Bacchus, formerly Director in charge of the Rover-Honda relationship

In the mid-1970s, I was Strategic Planning Director for BL International. I'd been watching Honda for some time; I found them fascinating because their US performance was astonishing. They had come from nowhere and now a Honda franchise was the absolute prize in the USA. They were also very advanced in their design as compared with their Japanese counterparts.

When Michael Edwardes took over, we quickly realized that collaboration was the way forward. This was unheard-of in the industry, at least among the major players, even though it has since become common. A sensible choice at the time looked like an alliance with Chrysler Europe, who were being supported by the government just as we were. Then, before we made an approach, Chrysler was sold to PSA Peugeot-Citroen! Honda was our choice as a replacement collaborator.

Michael Edwardes knew Sir Fred Warner, the former British Ambassador to Tokyo, and he suggested getting him to make the initial approach to Honda. Years later, a senior Honda man told me that this had been a master-stroke: the Honda Board (correctly) assumed an approach through such a man indicated that the plan must have the backing of the British Government!

Just eighteen months into the Honda relationship, we were talking about the joint executive car project. We started out with great optimism, but things became difficult almost straight away. A difficulty was our self-perception. We knew all about executive cars and Honda didn't, but what we knew was how to build them in the old 'blacksmith' way, which was common in Western industry at the time.

Another problem was working out who was responsible for engineering what. We aimed for greater commonality than we achieved, but we wanted to maximize local content for obvious reasons. Then we had problems with our suppliers, because they couldn't achieve the quality we needed at the prices we were prepared to pay. The tales of woe came up at Board meetings, and I remember Les Wharton saying to me that he couldn't understand it; what was going wrong? Sadly, I knew I was on safe ground when I told him that every problem component on the 800 and all the quality issues were our responsibility.

It was poor quality that pushed Honda to ask for an end to the original agreement that had us building Hondas at Cowley and them building Rovers in Japan. They were very tactful about it, but there was no way of sweetening the pill. Then it was quality again that was largely responsible for us pulling Sterling out of the USA a few years later.

It was heartbreaking. UK engineering and manufacturing were letting us down. But on the bright side, the collaboration with Honda gave us a very good car which stood us in good stead, and we learned a lot which was applied with great success to the Concerto/R8 programme a few years later.

Wootton Wawen,
April 2016

CHAPTER ONE

GENESIS

By the time work began on the Rover 800 project in the early 1980s, the old Rover Company had long since ceased to exist. Since 1975, Rover had simply been one of many traditional British marque names that belonged to the Leyland Cars division of the nationalized British Leyland.

The rot had set in during the mid-1960s. Rover was a small car manufacturer, and as other British manufacturers grouped together for strength, it sought shelter with the Leyland truck and bus group, which already owned Standard-Triumph. From 1968, at government instigation, the Leyland group joined forces with British Motor Holdings, formed in 1966 when Jaguar had merged with the old British Motor Corporation, which owned Austin, Morris and many other marques. The result was the British Leyland Motor Corporation (BLMC).

For a time, BLMC left Rover to its own devices, but by 1971 rationalization was in the air. The Rover and Triumph operations were amalgamated under the Rover-Triumph banner, and not long after that a further reorganization saw them becoming part of BL's Specialist Division along with Land Rover and Jaguar. In parallel, the less prestigious marques were amalgamated as the Volume Cars Division; in practice, by this time it had been reduced to the three marques of Austin, Morris and MG.

Generally speaking, the buying public remained blissfully unaware, perhaps uninterested, as the once fascinatingly diverse British motor industry was radically slimmed down. It was only when British Leyland ran out of money at the end of 1974 and turned to the government for help that most Britons sat up and took an interest. The reasons for the BL collapse were multiple and are well enough known. When the government stepped in to nationalize the company in order to save jobs, the car manufacturing side was renamed Leyland Cars.

As far as the Rover name was concerned, it still stood for luxury cars, although its original association with top build quality and discreet conservatism had been badly eroded during the 1970s. As Leyland Cars implemented its recovery plan towards the end of that decade, there was no new Rover in the offing because the SD1 saloon (introduced in 1976) was still relatively new. However, from 1979, Jaguar Rover Triumph did begin to look at a project called Bravo, which was a reskinned SD1 with both four-door and five-door derivatives and a range of engines from 2-litre O-series through 2.6-litre straight-six up to the 3.5-litre V8. At that stage, there was no money to look at anything more ambitious.

Bravo did not last long as the planned SD1 replacement. Jaguar Rover Triumph was dissolved in 1980 and a new Light-Medium Cars division of BL Cars was established. The new product plan included a car known as LM15, an enlarged Montego derivative now intended as the SD1 replacement. But before this could become firmly established as a project, the idea of building the new big Rover jointly with Honda swam into view. Shortly after that, a further reorganization of the business in 1982 saw BL Cars become Austin Rover, and many older marques were allowed to wither away. So it was Austin Rover that was really the parent of the Rover 800 – and in 1986, there would be yet another reorganization of the business that would see the company renamed as the Rover Group.

So what led the Rover 800 to be a Rover at all? The thinking at the time was that it was a large saloon from the rump of the British Leyland group that fitted a space in the market traditionally occupied by the Rover brand. Yet a traditional Rover it was not: it had no carry-over engineering from earlier Rover models; it was not designed or engineered by any of the leading lights of the old Rover Company; and it was not even built at a Rover factory. In its use of front-wheel drive, it was more Austin than Rover. For all that, it could not have been an Austin; it was aimed too far up the market for that. As a Rover, it benefited from the long-standing Rover image and tradition, and from the goodwill that the Rover brand had accrued in its independent heyday.

As a Rover, it could also be sold at a higher price than any Austin – and Austin Rover still needed every penny it could make.

BL AND HONDA

By the end of the 1970s, the global market for new cars seemed to be shrinking, and manufacturers everywhere began to look long and hard at their future prospects. The second oil crisis in 1979 also made clear that new kinds of cars would be needed in the future – cars that used less fuel and yet offered the levels of performance and creature comforts that customers already expected. It was a tall order, and several car manufacturers came to the same conclusion at about the same time. They needed to create strategic alliances, to share expertise and development costs, and to develop new cars as collaborative projects until things settled down.

Leyland Cars (as it then was) was in the middle of a hugely expensive recovery plan under Sir Michael Edwardes, with the Metro, the Montego and the Maestro all in the pipeline as new Austin products for the early 1980s. Yet these new cars would not fill all of the company's product requirements. More products were needed, quickly and cheaply, and as a result Leyland began talks with the Japanese Honda company in 1979.

Honda meant little in Europe and wanted to expand its presence in that market; it realized that it could best do so by forming an alliance with a company that had that expertise, and by learning from it. From Rover's point of view, Honda was an ideal partner because it had reliable and well-engineered products that it was willing to make available for licence production. So in 1979 the two companies agreed to begin working together, and the first visible indication of this was the introduction in 1981 of the Triumph Acclaim. The car was nothing more than a Honda Ballade, Europeanized a little to make it suitable for its new market, built under licence in the UK, and rebadged. Honda were already learning, and Leyland Cars had a strong (if unexciting) and thoroughly reliable new small car to sell.

Two years later, the BL–Honda alliance produced a second Japanese car, which was badged as a Rover, although in this case it was seen only in Australia. That car was the Rover Quintet, a Japanese-built Honda Quint with Rover badges. Its five-door hatchback style gave it a plausible family relationship to the Rover SD1, which was then still on sale,

but it was not really a Rover of any sort. A year later, though, the replacement for the Triumph Acclaim heralded a new era for Rover. The Rover 200 series, introduced in 1984, was the fruit of greater engineering cooperation between the two companies. Basically a second-generation Honda Ballade, it had been heavily restyled by Austin Rover engineers and given an Austin engine as one of its powerplants.

While all this was going on, the company that would become Austin Rover in 1982 was gradually taking shape. The old Triumph operation was closed down in stages, with TR7 sports car manufacture moving into Rover's Solihull factory during 1980 and the Triumph Dolomite medium-saloon range ending production to make way for the new Honda-derived Acclaim in 1981. Triumph's Canley premises became the Austin Rover headquarters, and the design studios for the whole group moved into the former Triumph parts and sales building. As 1981 slid into 1982, Rover car manufacture moved from its established Solihull home to the old Morris works at Cowley. The next new Rover, the 200 series of 1984, was built at the former Austin works in Longbridge. It was clear that the old boundaries and taboos had been overturned.

There were changes at the helm during 1982, as well. In the autumn of that year, Sir Michael Edwardes' five-year contract expired and he disappeared from the picture, leaving a management team of his own choosing to carry on the work he had begun. British Leyland would now

Roy Axe had overall responsibility for the visual elements of the Rover 800. He is pictured here with a full-size model of the four-door car.

consist of two groups. One was Land Rover-Leyland and would incorporate those two marques; it was headed by David Andrews. The other was the Cars Group, headed by Ray Horrocks, and Austin Rover was part of this; other elements were Jaguar (which was managed separately), BL Technology, and the Unipart spares operation.

Ray Horrocks had been BL's managing director under Edwardes. Under him as chairman of Austin Rover now came Harold Musgrove, the former managing director of the Austin Morris division. Bill Horton became Austin Rover's technical director and Mark Snowdon its managing director. In charge of Design (formerly known as Styling) was Roy (Royden) Axe, who had come in from Chrysler when Rover's David Bache had been summarily dismissed after a row with Harold Musgrove.

JOINT DESIGN

It was against this background that the Rover–Honda alliance moved smoothly forward. In the autumn of 1981 it reached an important milestone. After a preliminary meeting in September that year, the two companies signed a letter of intent on 12 November for the joint design, development and manufacture of a new large car. For BL Cars (soon to be Austin Rover), the deal would provide a replacement for the Rover SD1; on the Honda side, it would give the company a credible product in the large-saloon class where it had never before competed, and without the risks associated with a tentative first attempt.

The initiative had come from Austin Rover, but Honda had proved cautious at first. Sir Michael Edwardes recalled the British company's approach in an interview for *Motor* magazine dated 9 August 1986:

> When we first raised the possibility of a truly international joint venture car with Mr Kiyoshi Kawashima, chairman of Honda, he was at that stage reluctant to commit Honda to such an ambitious project.
>
> I believe that particular meeting was in Anchorage, Alaska, and it was difficult to fault his logic. The Triumph Acclaim project was already under way – it had been signed in Tokyo in December 1979 – and he felt we should feel confident that the two companies could prove their ability to work together before embarking on the much more ambitious project that was eventually to lead to this new Rover.

This was to be a groundbreaking deal in more ways than one. It kick-started the first-ever joint project between two car manufacturers to plan, design, engineer and manufacture a car. The project would be massively complicated as there would be both Honda and Rover derivatives of the car, each one differently styled to suit its manufacturer's requirements but both sharing the same inner structure. Powertrains and suspension would also be shared by both derivatives, and – perhaps most difficult of all – the cars had to be engineered so that Rover derivatives could be built alongside their Honda siblings on the Honda production line at Sayama in Japan while Honda derivatives could be built alongside Rovers on the British production line at Cowley.

At the same time as the top management from BL and Honda signed their letter of intent in November, the two companies' design teams met to make a start on the project. It became clear very early on that there could be no carry-over engineering from earlier Rovers. Both Honda and the Austin side of the British company were wedded to transverse engines and front-wheel drive, so it was inevitable that the new car would have such a configuration. Honda were committed to building a new V6 engine for transverse installation; for the Japanese domestic market, this would have a 2-litre capacity, but for export markets there would be a more powerful 2.5-litre version. Austin Rover would take this engine for the top models of the new car, but they already had a range of engines designed for front-wheel-drive applications, and they chose to use further-developed versions of these as the smaller-capacity engines in the new model. That they were fundamentally Austin engines was of no consequence, except, perhaps, to Rover diehards who were already wincing at the thought of Rover badges on a car designed partially in Japan.

From a very early stage, it was also clear that the car would have to be a four-door saloon. This was what Honda wanted, and Rover's market research had indicated that it was what large-car buyers in their markets wanted, too. However, a substantial proportion of Rover buyers had been impressed by the hatchback configuration of the SD1, so Rover earmarked a five-door hatchback derivative of the new car for later development. When a concept submission for the new car was put up to Rover management in 1982, it included not only a hatchback derivative but also a two-door coupé; Honda had no interest in a hatchback but, unbeknown to the Rover team, they were also interested in developing a two-door coupé. Both companies also wanted to sell the car in the USA; Rover intended to make

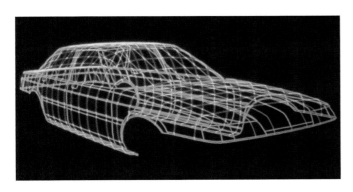

Computer-aided design was still in its early stages when XX was being drawn up. This picture shows an outline of the body-in-white, the metal elements of the four-door body.

a comeback there after pulling their SD1 out of the market somewhat ignominiously in 1981.

BODY DESIGN

Once the new joint project had been approved by the management of both companies, the designers and engineers got down to work. From the start, it was agreed that the common language on the project would be English – although in practice many of the British engineers involved ended up learning Japanese as well. Regular communication by telephone and fax would be backed up by regular visits by each engineering team to the other, so that there would be no misunderstandings. Fundamentally, however, the project could not have worked without a huge amount of goodwill by the engineers on both sides, and it is to their credit that such a pioneering venture became a major success.

On the Rover side, Derek Peck was appointed overall project director. An initial division of responsibilities was drawn up, with Honda agreeing to develop the V6 engine; the manual and automatic gearboxes to go with it; the brakes; the interior trim; and the heating, ventilating and air-conditioning systems. Rover meanwhile agreed to develop the bodyshell, making particular use of the expertise in computer-aided design that they had acquired in recent years and which was the envy of the Japanese. They would also develop the suspension, and would of course be solely responsible for further development of the Austin engines that they wanted in order to expand the range downwards. All projects end up with code names, both for convenience

and for secrecy, and the new Rover was given the name Project XX. The Honda derivative was known as Project HX.

As the bodyshell was fundamental to the whole project, Roy Axe's team at Canley began sketching up ideas around the 'hard points' agreed with Honda early in 1982. These included a wheelbase of 108.3in (2,750mm) – shorter than the 110.8in (2,814mm) of the SD1, but also shorter than the production size for reasons that will become apparent later. A critical dimension for Honda was an overall width of no more than 66.9in (1,700mm); above that, cars in Japan were subject to tax penalties.

Some ideas were already in place. Roy Axe and his team were particularly interested in the design trends that had emerged at the Frankfurt Motor Show in autumn 1981, then the most recent of the major shows and a useful pointer for their own future design work. What that show had made clear was that most European designers saw aerodynamic designs as the future. As Axe explained in an interview for *Autocar* magazine of 10 July 1986:

> *The question was whether we wanted to jump into that pot, steer clear of it, or take account of it; in the end, we decided to take account of it, and I felt very strongly between us that we could give the sort of totally competitive aerodynamic performance we wanted, but not make the design look as if it had been designed in a wind tunnel – that was not what we wanted.*

'Apart from this,' he added, 'we wanted to give continuity to the new company identity which had been started quite well in SD1. Looks have never been a problem for SD1.'

The British design team began work on the shape of the body before their Japanese colleagues, and the first sketches were done in January 1982. At this stage, there was an understanding that the two cars would share a centre section and that Rover and Honda derivatives would be differentiated by their front and rear end designs. As Axe told *Autocar* in that July 1986 interview, 'We chose continuity, a balance between aerodynamics and sporting appeal – very strong in SD1. The car needed to be elegant.' Chief exterior designer on the project, Gordon Sked, emphasized that point. 'There is no place for the executive car that is not elegant,' he said.

Gordon Sked's choice from among the early concept sketches very much set the style for XX. There was no

Although it was clear that XX would have to be a four-door model, some quite radical designs were put forward by members of the design team.

The idea of a flattened off rear wheel arch remained quite persistent in early exterior design renderings. The chiselled, six-light shape is already clear in this one.

The contrasting lower flank panels were clearly intended as a way of protecting against bumps, but the idea was later followed through in the contrasting lower paintwork options for the Sterling.

disagreement about this, as he later explained: 'Roy and I always wanted a six-light glass configuration with wrap-around A-post and the continuous line at belt height from nose to tail, unbroken by the A-post.' So the chosen design was taken forward to be turned into a full-size mock-up. This was certainly aerodynamic, with sharp, angular lines, half-spats over the rear wheels, and a Cd of just 0.27. As seen from above, it had barrel-shaped sides, and there was a pronounced crab track. However, the designers felt that the small front and back made the car look too small overall, and that the narrow rear track adversely affected boot space and fuel tank size. The initial design was therefore developed further, and an evolutionary full-size clay model was ready by July 1982. The appearance of this second design coincided with the start of Honda's work on their body styling.

The Rover design had evolved further by September 1982, when the new full-size model from Roy Axe's team took on the designation DEV1. It still had those aerodynamic half-spats over the rear wheels, and it had a narrower middle section with wider front and rear ends while retaining some of the original convex shape. An interesting feature of the design was thermostatic grille shutters, reflecting the dominance at this stage of aerodynamic thinking.

At Austin Rover's Canley studios, the next stage was the full-size DEV2 mock-up, completed in November 1982 in glass-reinforced plastic (GRP). This had lost the half-spats and now had part-circular wheel-arch openings. It had an appearance that one of the designers told *Autocar* was 'sweeping, more aerodynamic and softer', and the windscreen had quite a steep rake with deep side wrap-arounds.

Roy Axe and Gordon Sked agreed that the balance and proportion of the latest design were right but that the car

The flattened rear wheel arch was still in the thinking when this model was constructed for aerodynamic tests, carried out in the wind tunnel at MIRA.

This full-size model again shows the flattened rear wheel arch. The lines have clear definition, although they would sadly be toned down somewhat before production began.

... and here is the toned-down version, still as a full-size mock-up. The rear wheel arch is now round, but the model seems to sit lower than production versions ever did, and looks all the better for it. The contrasting colour for the lower flank panels is evident here.

One of the model-makers adjusting the lines of a full-size model, which is close to the finished version. This is a 'solid' model: the windows are represented by Dynoc film.

This full-size, see-through model was photographed in the 'viewing garden' at Canley, and shows the final version of XX as approved for production. The wheel trims indicate that this particular model represents a derivative with the mid-range level of trim and equipment.

still looked 'a bit too soft' and too small. They wanted to increase the perception of size, by making the boot bigger; ideally, they would also have liked a longer wheelbase. That windscreen design would also have presented problems for the glass manufacturers, and ensuring that it did not pop out in the US barrier-crash test would also have been difficult.

The DEV2 GRP model was shipped to Tokyo during November so that it could be viewed by the management of both companies alongside the Honda equivalent. However, it was becoming clear at this stage that divergences between the Honda design and the Austin Rover design were likely to lead to problems. So the decision was made to abandon the idea of a common centre section and different front and rear ends. Instead, each side would develop its own body design around a common floorpan, engine bay and body structure. However, it would be vitally important that the progress of

the two designs should be monitored very closely, to catch any critical divergences before they became problems.

As a result, the Honda and Rover full-size clays were brought together at Canley in January 1983 and were developed side by side. The experience fostered good links and additional respect between the British and Japanese design teams, and the facia panel designs being drawn up at this stage were done on a complementary basis. The Austin Rover exterior design evolved during this period into DEV3. This tackled the windscreen issue that had arisen with DEV2 by moving the base of the screen rearwards, making it flatter and with less wrap-around. The longer bonnet helped to alter the size perception of the car, and this mock-up was now very close in appearance to the final production design.

While the designers created the exterior style, the body engineers kept a close eye on developments to ensure that the inner structure of the shell really would suit both Honda and Rover designs. There were therefore several common elements: these included the floorpan, the bulkheads, the inner body sides, the ducting for the heater system and the suspension pick-up points. As for the construction of the shell, the engineers chose to go with 'monosides', in which each side section from the front bulkhead rearwards is made as a single pressing.

The idea of angling the centre stack towards the driver took hold early on. There is a somewhat geometric theme to these interior proposals – and the left-hand-drive one (dated December 1981) shows a profusion of steering-wheel controls, which was an advanced idea for the time.

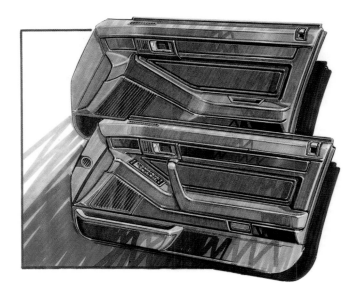

The geometric theme persisted in these proposals for interior door panel designs.

TOP RIGHT: **This hard model of the dashboard looks a little cluttered but features a lot of new ideas. Note the graphic display on the instrument panel and, once again, several control buttons on the steering wheel.**

MIDDLE RIGHT: **Looking remarkably realistic, even down to the textures of the materials, this is a late mock-up of the XX dashboard.**

ABOVE: **The interior design is here being translated into a full-size buck in the studios at Canley ...**

... and here is another full-size interior buck, this time in finished condition. There would have been several of these, each representing a different set of proposals.

THE ENGINES

The front end of the bodyshell was of course designed to leave room for all the planned engines. The intention was to mount each of these on an H-shaped subframe, which could be modified relatively easily if engine changes became necessary later.

Honda's V6 Engine

Honda drew up their new V6 as an all-alloy engine with cast-iron cylinder liners, and in order to reduce its overall height chose to use a 90-degree angle between the cylinder banks instead of the 60-degree angle more commonly seen on V6 designs. This low height was important to them because a very low bonnet line had become something of a Honda trademark.

Honda wanted two different sizes of this V6 engine, a 2-litre for the Japanese domestic market and a larger 2.5-litre for export. These were known as the C20A and C25A types respectively, and the larger size was earmarked for use in the top models of the Rover derivative. The original Honda plan was for a 3-valve design. Austin Rover's engineers questioned the wisdom of this at an early stage, suggesting that power and torque might not be enough; that the block might be unable to take the cylinder pressures; and that the uneven combustion chamber design might lead to detonation problems. However, the Japanese pressed ahead

with their original design and, as Derek Peck told *Motor* magazine in its 12 July 1986 issue, 'they kept the engine design very close to their chests.' This would cause problems later in the development programme.

The design went ahead with crankpins offset by 30 degrees and a single overhead camshaft on each cylinder bank, driven by a toothed rubber belt to minimize noise and operating the valves through fingers and short pushrods, with hydraulic tappets to minimize servicing requirements. Fuel delivery was controlled by Honda's PGM-FI system, those letters standing for Programmed Fuel Injection. The design incorporated a significant concession to the Rover side in that Honda agreed to make the crankshaft rotate in the conventional (clockwise) direction; earlier Honda car engines had been notable for their anticlockwise rotation.

Austin Rover's Smaller Petrol Engines

Like Honda, Austin Rover wanted alternatives to the 2.5-litre V6 engine intended for the flagship cars, but they decided to use their own engines. So the smaller-capacity Rover engines were derived from the Austin-Morris O-series 4-cylinder, a generally reliable powerplant perhaps best known from its appearance in the Austin Princess (later Ambassador) saloons. Further development under the company's engines guru, Roland Bertodo, focused on lightening and refining the O-series block, and on marrying it to a new alloy 4-valve cylinder head derived from that used on the 16-valve Triumph Dolomite Sprint engine. (For completists, this was perhaps a link back to the old days of Rover, because the ingenious valve gear design of that engine had been drawn up by Rover's Spen King after he had been put in charge of Triumph under British Leyland.) In the fashion of the time, the new M16 engine's single overhead camshaft was driven by a toothed rubber belt.

Rover chose to develop this engine in two different states of tune for the XX, not least because their aim was to replace the three models – 2000, 2300 and 2600 – that had sat below the flagship 3500 models in the SD1 range. So they chose two different injection systems to do so. The less powerful derivative of the M16 engine (known as the M16e and developing 120PS/118bhp) had single-point throttle-body injection developed by Austin Rover's own engineers. The more powerful derivative (the M16i with 140PS/138bhp) used a bought-in Lucas L-type hot-wire multi-point injection system, which was also used on the MG Montego EFi.

THROTTLE-BODY INJECTION

The throttle-body injection system used on the M16 2-litre engine in the 820E and 820SE cars was developed wholly within the Austin Rover Group, and the cars became the first ones manufactured in Britain to use such a system. A key advantage of throttle-body injection was that it was cheaper to manufacture than a multi-point injection system. Although it did not bring all the advantages of those more sophisticated systems, it did allow precise metering of fuel. This in turn delivered good accelerator response, good cold start performance and good fuel economy.

Out of the car, the throttle-body injection engine looked like this. The picture is taken from the back of the engine, which was normally hidden from view.

This is the rear view of the multi-point injection engine. Note the distinctive curved inlet tracts.

Diesel XX

Rover also needed a diesel engine to meet demand in Europe, where the 2400SD Turbo version of the SD1 had won them good sales in the large-saloon market. A diesel was a step too far for Honda, so Rover were left to go it alone on this one. However, the British company had more than enough on their hands at this stage, so the diesel XX was treated as a separate development project. As a result, the model did not become available until four years after the XX had entered production. It was a delay that probably cost Rover valuable sales.

TRANSMISSION AND 'CHASSIS' DESIGN

Transmission

The manual gearboxes would be five-speeds designed by Honda. There were two types, the PG1 for the 2-litre engines and the stronger PG2 for the 2.5-litre size. The PG1 was in fact integrated into Austin Rover's manufacturing programme some two years before it was needed for XX production as it had been introduced for the 2-litre versions of the Austin Montego in 1984. Honda had agreed to engineer the gearbox early and to lay down extra capacity to build it for the Montego, which was a strong indication of their willingness to collaborate quite broadly with Austin Rover. In practice, Austin Rover were able to negotiate an agreement to build the gearbox under licence at Longbridge. It would remain in production there until 2005 and would be used in a variety of Rover Group models, including the Land Rover Freelander. The version of the PG1 adopted for the 2-litre versions of the new Rover nevertheless had different ratios from the one in the Montego.

Honda also designed the automatic to go behind their V6 engine, using an unusual two-shaft design with electronic control and a torque converter lock to reduce power losses. For the 2-litre versions of the Austin Rover car, however, the British company chose a four-speed gearbox made by ZF in Germany. This was the 4HP 14 type, which also featured a lock-up for the torque converter in top gear and partial lock-up in third gear. Like the PG1 manual gearbox, it had already been seen on the car maker's 2-litre Austin Montego.

Suspension, Steering and Brakes

Suspension design involved some compromises. The Austin Rover team felt that strut front suspension would be fine, but Honda were absolutely set on using a double-wishbone set-up, which they felt would be more appropriate for a luxury car. The compromise was to use both struts and a double-wishbone design, which the Austin Rover engineers accepted rather grudgingly. It had two disadvantages, as far as they were concerned: first, it was expensive; second, it limited wheel travel and therefore compromised the ride quality.

The British team did get its own way with the rear suspension. Initially, the Japanese had again wanted a wishbone layout, but they accepted the British argument that struts would save space and so allow a larger boot. As Austin Rover also had plans to develop a hatchback model later, extra width between the wheel arches was an important consideration for them. To prevent the car from dragging its tail when the boot was loaded, thus compromising the handling, the plan was to fit a Boge Nivomat self-levelling strut. This became standard on the top two Rover models (the 825i and 825 Sterling), but was not made an extra-cost option on others.

As this was to be a luxury car, power-assisted steering would have to be standard, but in practice the Austin Rover engineers chose two different types. One was a speed-proportional Honda design, which Honda planned to use on their own car and was always used for the V6 models. For the 4-cylinder cars, however, the British engineers developed their own Positive Centre Feel (PCF) system, which was manufactured for them by Cam Gears.

Brakes were to have ventilated front discs (with different sizes on the Rover for the 4-cylinder and V6 cars), and with ABS (Anti-lock Braking System) availability. In practice, ABS was made standard only on the top-model Rover.

DEVELOPMENT AND PROTOTYPES

With the basic design work completed by the end of 1983, the next two years were to be devoted to development and testing. During 1984, the first XX prototypes were smashed against solid barriers at the Motor Industry Research Association (MIRA) to evaluate their crash performance characteristics; others went on high-mileage endurance tests to see what would break or wear out too quickly; and the designers began to look to the future.

There was one further major borrowing from Honda in this period, and that was the Japanese company's prototype build system. The Austin Rover tradition had been to proceed from engineering 'mules' (existing models with some of the planned new elements grafted onto them) to semi-engineered prototypes and then to pilot production models built using production tooling. Honda's system was quite different and relied on greater numbers of prototypes created over nine stages. Each stage might involve as many as twenty cars, which gave a potential total of around 180 prototype vehicles; for comparison, there had probably been around twenty-five prototypes of the SD1, plus a large number of pilot-production cars. In practice, there were probably no more than seventy-five prototypes of the XX.

The Honda system consisted of three major stages, each of which had three substages. The first stages were for research, and were called R01, R02 and R03. The second stages were for development (D01, D02 and D03). Finally, the pilot-build stages were called TRY1, TRY2 and TRY3. The great advantage of this system was that there were always enough prototypes to be allocated to the different departments involved so that they could all do their development work simultaneously instead of having to wait for another department to finish their work before getting access to a car.

Some of the XX prototypes were caught by 'scoop' photographers working for the motoring press, although those that went out on test wore a very heavy disguise, which made it impossible to make out their real shape. By the time *Motor* magazine was able to publish a photograph of a car on test, in its issue dated 20 October 1984, the word was already out that the car would be introduced as a four-door saloon and the magazine was able to publish a quite accurate line drawing of the way the production car would look. Nevertheless, the heavily camouflaged test car was mocked up to look like a five-door hatchback, and photographs in the Austin Rover archives confirm that this was a favourite disguise.

By this stage, the XX project had already been hit by a major problem, but dedicated work from Roy Axe's team had overcome it so that the overall timing of the project was not affected. From the early stages, Rover engineers had entertained doubts about the Japanese plans for the

These photographs, dated 21 November 1984, show a disguised **XX** prototype. Although the basic lines can be picked out, the detail is very unclear – and that was the intention. At least one similarly disguised car was caught on test at the Gaydon proving ground by a scoop photographer, and the results were published. However, it was impossible to tell whether the car under the camouflage was a five-door or a four-door with a dummy hatchback.

new V6 engine. They were concerned that the 3-valve design would fail to deliver the necessary power and torque and that the uneven combustion chamber design associated with it would give trouble. They believed that the block and head design that the Japanese were working on was not strong enough for the job, and project director Derek Peck had made Rover's concerns quite clear.

It was (and still is) a Japanese cultural trait never to admit

that there may be a problem, something that the Rover engineers encountered over and over again during the development stages of XX. The Japanese way of admitting that the Rover engineers' concerns had been justified was to announce, in June 1984, that they were making changes to the V6 engine. Testing had indeed shown up weaknesses in the cylinder block and heads, but all would now be well because a redesign was under way.

Early production or pre-production 800s are seen here on a test rig, which replicated in a matter of days the amount of vibration they would encounter in a lifetime.

The new design would not only incorporate four valves per cylinder instead of three, but would also make the engine wider, longer and 0.2in (5mm) taller — a decision that had enormous consequences for the size of the engine bay, which was already tightly packed. Nevertheless, the Honda engineers had the first prototypes of the revised engine ready within five months — an astounding turnaround time in view of the complexity of the changes involved.

While that redesign was going ahead, the Rover engineers looked at the implications of the new and larger engine bay. First, an additional 0.35in (9mm) had to be inserted between front bulkhead and front wheel arch — so extending the wheelbase. Then the wheels had to be moved outwards by 5.4in (120mm), giving a wider front track. Not only was the engineering affected, but so was the body design: 'It totally changed every surface forward of the A-post and wind-screen rail, coming very late in the day,' one of the designers told *Autocar* in July 1986.

Roy Axe's design team coped with this very quickly, having a modified front end ready within six weeks. In fact, it worked to their advantage, allowing them to put back a little of the aerodynamic plan form that had been lost in earlier stages of the design. They redesigned the front wings to accommodate the wider track and matched everything up to the existing shape. By contrast, the Japanese team took an easier way out, adding wheel-arch blisters to the front of their car and matching these with sculpted shapes on the rear wings.

LOOKING TO THE FUTURE

Roy Axe's designers began to look at future developments

of the XX from an early stage. A two-door coupé derivative had been in the plan since the beginning, and early in 1984 Axe asked his designers to get started on sketching ideas. Rover also wanted a five-door hatchback derivative of the car to satisfy customers who had liked that aspect of the SD1 design, so work began on that as well. Then, as an unexpected development during the year, the design studio was asked to come up with a stretched-wheelbase car to sell to customers who wanted a limousine.

This was brought about by the sale of Jaguar into private ownership. Austin Rover management wanted to look at competing with the long-wheelbase Jaguars, which were now potential rivals, and hoped that a long-wheelbase derivative of the XX might fit the bill. Axe's team drew up a model with an extra 15in (380mm) in the wheelbase, all of it accommodated in the rear door area, and took their design as far as a full-size mock-up. Though it was undoubtedly an elegant design, it was not taken forward to production. Instead, the long-wheelbase limousine market was left to aftermarket converters such as Coleman Milne (see Chapter 9).

It looks as if some even more interesting ideas for the future were being investigated during 1985. *Motor* magazine's issue dated 10 August reported that the Austrian specialists Steyr-Daimler-Puch were working on a four-wheel-drive derivative of the XX. This was not as unrealistic as it initially sounds: Audi had made a big splash by using four-wheel drive in their 1981 Quattro coupé, and both Mercedes-Benz and BMW had developed 4x4 versions of their saloon and estate cars to suit customers who lived in snowy Alpine regions of Europe, and to meet a similar demand in the USA.

Austin Rover were not to be drawn on the subject, how-

The privatization of Jaguar in 1984 prompted Austin Rover to investigate a long-wheelbase limousine version of the XX. This is it in mock-up form at Canley, displaying very well-proportioned lines.

ever. Joe Farnham, by then director of product engineering, told *Motor* that 'if the customer demands 4WD then they will get it from Austin Rover'. He did add that such a car would need a new floorpan, because 'if you start with a front-wheel-drive design for 4WD you lose all the packaging advantage of the original design'. One way or another, nothing more was heard of this development, and its existence has never been confirmed.

The original plan had been for the Rover 800 and its Japanese equivalent – the Honda Legend – to be launched at the same time, but Japanese superiority in production engineering allowed them to have their car ready for sale a full nine months before the Rover. The Honda Legend was introduced at the Tokyo Motor Show on 22 October 1985.

In order to head off awkward questions about the related Rover model, Austin Rover held a special press briefing at Canley that month. It became clear at the briefing that there had been around sixty-eight prototypes of the new Rover – although nothing was said about how many additional prototypes Honda might have built. The forthcoming top model was described as a Vanden Plas, so presumably the eventual

production name (Sterling) had not at that stage been chosen – or perhaps it had, and the briefing was deliberately misleading so that the new name would have more impact when it arrived for real. It would do exactly that in July 1986.

KEY DATES

1981, 12 November	Austin Rover and Honda sign a joint development and production memorandum for a new large executive car.
1983, 6 April	The two companies sign a formal joint development agreement.
1984, 17 April	Signing of a joint production agreement.
1985, 22 October	Honda Legend announced in Japan.
1986, 10 July	Rover 800 announced in UK.

WHY 'ROVER 800'?

Austin Rover developed a new system of naming its products, mainly as a way of making its range appear more integrated. So although the Rovers that the XX would replace had numbers indicative of their engine size (2000, 2600, 3500 and so on) and Austin practice had been to use names (such as Montego and Maestro), from 1984 things would begin to change.

There is little doubt that the new system had been inspired by the clear brand identification and stratification achieved by the ultra-successful BMW brand. The German car maker identified its saloon ranges by a simple numerical system. Its compact entry-level saloon in the 1980s was the 3 Series (becoming a 320 with a 2-litre engine, a 325 with a 2.5-litre engine and so on). Above that, the medium-sized saloon was called the 5 Series, and right at the top of the range was the 7 Series luxury saloon.

The new Austin Rover system was introduced in July 1984 with the Rover 200 – successor to the Triumph Acclaim in the small-saloon sector of the market and essentially a Honda Ballade with modified looks and some British-built engines. The number 800 was chosen for the Rover flagship, leaving enough numbers in between for new models that would later build up the complete range. Like BMW, Austin Rover identified individual models by adding numbers that showed the engine size. So the 1.3-litre Rover 200 was called a 213 and the 1.6-litre type a Rover 216. The same system would be used for the 800 range, the 2-litre models taking the Rover 820 name and the 2.5-litre models bearing Rover 825 badges. Suffix letters would identify sub-variants.

In practice, it would be some years before the new naming strategy became clear. The original Rover 200 had already been replaced in 1989 by a second-generation car with the same name before the Rover 400 appeared in 1990 as a variant of this. It would then be three more years before the Rover 600 rounded out the range, and 1994 before a facelifted version of the Austin (latterly Rover) Metro became a Rover 100. The names of Rover 100, 200, 400, 600 and 800 continued until the late 1990s, when the Rover Group adopted another new naming system, starting with the Rover 75 in 1998.

CHAPTER TWO

THE FIRST 800 SERIES MODELS, 1986–1988

Austin Rover orchestrated a careful build-up to the availability of the new 800 Series cars in the UK. Although details and pictures of the cars carried a press embargo until 10 July 1986, the media pack was issued as early as 22 May. It was followed less than a week later by a separate release about a new laser measuring rig for checking body dimensions that had been installed at the Cowley works. Although the 800 was not specifically mentioned, it was clear that this rig was intended to ensure high quality of manufacture in the eagerly anticipated new Rover.

The cooperation with Honda was well known, and Honda had a reputation for building efficient if somewhat soulless medium-sized and small cars. So it was important to allay any fears among potential customers that the new Rover would not live up to the public image of its name. The launch material issued to the press was therefore at pains to point out that, 'despite the close cooperation [with Honda], Austin Rover has retained total control over the identity, image and parentage of its new Rover 800 executive car'.

It was also important to get across the message that the car was much more British than might be immediately apparent. So the launch release stressed that by far the majority of those built would have the 2-litre M16 engine designed and built by Austin Rover at Longbridge, and that the average British content across the 800 range was no less than 91 per cent. This was reinforced by the news on 13 July that the car had been selected by the Design Centre as an example of good British design.

Volume assembly had begun in the spring, slowly at first but building up rapidly after the official launch in July. Pro-

Emphasizing the Rover heritage in an attempt to deflect criticism that might be forthcoming about the Japanese link, Rover displayed the new 800 at the Motor Show with a 1907 Rover. The two were also photographed together for this publicity photo.

The front view of the 800, in this case a French-market **V6** model, was sharp and attractive. Unfortunately, it lacked the presence that many customers expected of a Rover.

BELOW: **This rear view of an early Sterling shows very clearly the sculpted lines characteristic of the new Rover, as well as the model identification on the boot lid. Only the V6 models had twin tailpipes like this.**

duction volume from the Cowley plant was 750 cars per week over the summer, but a second shift was introduced on the assembly lines in the autumn (probably in November) enabling volume to be increased to 1,500 cars per week. That suggested an annual capacity of 75,000 or more cars – a figure that made interesting comparison with the 30–35,000 SDIs that Rover's Solihull factory had turned out each year in the early 1980s.

Clearly, expectations of the 800 were high, and there was an ambitious plan to sell the cars abroad. Within a year of the 800's launch, it would be on sale in nearly thirty different countries around the world, and Austin Rover had an even more ambitious plan to re-enter the US market with the 800 as its flagship product. The full story of that attempt is told in Chapter 5.

Austin Rover were very proud of their investment in state-of-the-art manufacturing at Cowley, where the 800 was built. Here, a left-hand-drive 2-litre model is put through an under-bonnet quality assurance check with a 'talking' computer.

I'LL BUILD YOURS, YOU BUILD MINE

From the start, the plan was that Rover would build Honda Legends in Britain for the UK and other European markets, while Honda would build Rover 800s in Japan for the Japanese and other Pacific markets. The cars were designed and engineered so that this could take place with the minimum of difficulty, but there were nevertheless differences between the Rover-built Hondas and the Honda-built Hondas, the Honda-built Rovers and the Rover-built Rovers.

The 800s built in Japan did not have the Bosch ABS system because this could not be accommodated on the Honda assembly line at Sayama, where production began in January 1987. Honda-built Rovers also had vertical-flow radiators instead of the cross-flow type, and the standard wheels were the spoked steel design used on Legends. The Honda Legends built in Britain had several items from the Rover's specification, including the 800's bigger brakes, cross-flow radiators and smaller and more sophisticated European batteries.

This element of the joint project was not very successful. The Japanese were not happy with the quality of the Rover-built Legends and after two years the cross-building arrangement came to an end. After November 1988, all Honda Legends were built in Japan and after December 1988 all Rover 800s were built in Britain.

THE LAUNCH MODELS

In theory, the 800 was launched in the UK with a six-model range, but in practice only the V6-engined cars were available in the beginning. A launch fleet of 1,000 825i and 825 Sterling models was built, supposedly all in silver and mostly with registration numbers in the Cxxx AAC series. Some of the Cxxx AAC cars were also reserved as early press demonstrators. In theory, there was supposed to be one demonstrator for each Rover showroom in the UK, but as there were 1,400 outlets the practice fell somewhat short of the theory. The 4-cylinder models followed after a gap of a few months, reaching showrooms in the autumn of 1986; automatic derivatives of the 2-litre cars were further delayed, until the end of the year.

That six-model range was made up by three engine variants, each with two levels of trim. So the entry-level M16e engine was available in models badged as 820E and 820SE; the more powerful M16i came in an 820i and an 820Si; and the Honda V6 came in an 825i and an 825 Sterling. The basic specification was quite generous, and all cars had electric front windows, electric mirrors, central locking, a rake-adjustable steering column, a stereo radio cassette system, and a radio aerial incorporated in the heated rear window elements.

The dark lower panels of the Sterling always made it tricky to photograph – especially in black and white, which was used for most press photos in the mid-1980s. This example shows the problem well.

Many of the cars used in the launch press photography wore registrations in the D-NTH series, which did not actually become road legal until August 1986 – some two months after the launch. This is an 825i, pictured at speed.

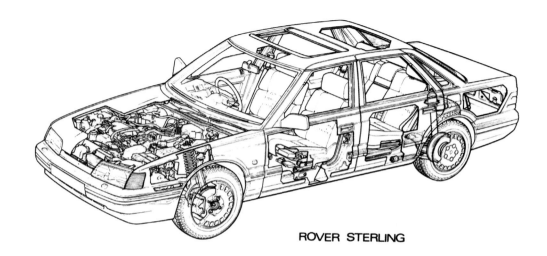

ROVER STERLING

This was the obligatory press-release cutaway, showing the essential elements of the 825 Sterling.

Colour press photographs were only available by special request, and here is one showing an **820Si** in the **D-NTH** registration series. Those polycarbonate wheel trims were used on all the steel-wheeled cars at the start of production.

Models with the entry-level 2-litre engine that featured throttle-body injection arrived a few months after the other models. This **820E** was dressed up with alloy wheels to distract attention from its otherwise somewhat plain-Jane appearance.

The interior of an 820i shows its standard fabric upholstery. The centre section of the rear bench is configured as a third seat, as on most Rover 800s.

The 820E, 820SE, 820i and 820Si

The entry-level 4-cylinder cars came with steel disc wheels concealed by silver polycarbonate trims with 'pepperpot' holes around the rim. The S-specification models also came with steel disc wheels, this time with polycarbonate trims that had a vane-like pattern on their outer rims. They also had a slim coachline at waist level, and bright trim on the waist rail. To these features were added remote infra-red central locking, a manually operated glass sunroof, electric rear windows, a courtesy lamp delay, a programmed wash-wipe, front reading lamps and a high-specification In-Car Entertainment (ICE) system. There were further extra features reserved for the V6 models, although many were also made available as extra-cost options on the 2-litre cars.

The 825i and Sterling

The two V6 models were recognizable from the front by a subtle bright strip across the air intake grille, a feature not seen on the 4-cylinder cars. The 825i came with head-lamp washers, a twin-exit stainless-steel exhaust pipe, a windscreen shade band, low-profile tyres on alloy wheels, a leather-rimmed steering wheel, different trim, individually adjustable rear seats, a trip computer, a vehicle warning system map and rear reading lamps. A sunroof and self-levelling rear suspension were all part of the specification.

Right at the top of the range, the Sterling was – claimed Austin Rover – the most highly specified production car ever to leave a British factory. To the 825i specification, it added two-tone paint (described as 'Duo Tone' in sales literature;

Leather upholstery was standard on the Sterling models. This picture shows quite clearly the way the backrest was arranged, with two separate side bolsters.

Rear seat passengers in the V6 models could have adjustable backrests, seen here with the fabric upholstery standard in an 825i. Note the head restraint associated with this option, and the way the rear seat was configured as two individual chairs with a panel in between.

The main dials on the dash were deliberately styled to look as if one overlapped the other. Auxiliary instruments flanked them.

in practice, a dark grey band around the lower body), ABS, unique alloy wheels, leather upholstery (cloth was optional), shag-pile overmats, electric front and rear seat adjusters (with a four-position memory for the driver's seat and door mirrors), air conditioning, an electric glass sunroof, cruise control and a top-specification ICE system.

THE STERLING NAME

The top models of the Rover SD1 that the 800 range replaced had carried Vanden Plas badges but the top models of the 800 range carried Sterling badges. Vanden Plas was an old-established coachbuilder whose British affiliate had been absorbed into the Austin empire in the late 1940s. The change seemed an odd thing to do at the time, but it was probably forced upon Austin Rover by the privatization of Jaguar in 1984. Jaguar had been using the Vanden Plas name on its top Daimler models, and retained the right to use it. Rover therefore had to think of something else – although it retained a residual right to use the Vanden Plas name on the SD1 models until their production ended in 1986. Rover was also granted permission to use the Vanden Plas name on a long-wheelbase version of the Rover 75 introduced in 2002.

The origin of the Sterling name remains unclear, but its associations were quite obvious. Sterling suggested the pound sterling, the British unit of currency, and the word had also come to mean 'reliable and praiseworthy' – a car might render sterling service to its owner, for example. The name would also be used instead of the Rover name when the 800 was launched into North America (see Chapter 5).

All the rational arguments were in favour of it. However, it lacked any history in the automotive world and to some ears therefore lacked credibility as the badge for the top-model Rover.

INITIAL PRESS REACTIONS

The press embargo for detailed information about the new Rovers was until 10 July 1986, by which time several members of the press had already flown out to Lausanne in Switzerland for the launch ride-and-drive event. There were examples with all three engines available for evaluation, although only the 820i, 820Si, 825i and 825 Sterling were to be available through showrooms initially. Austin Rover did point out that they were all pilot-production cars and that there might therefore be some minor deviations from production standard; that presumably excused what *Motor* (26 July 1986 issue) called the 'less than flawless detail finish on our early build test car'.

Over the next couple of weeks, a rash of articles featuring both driving impressions and the background to the XX design appeared in the UK motoring press. Generally speaking, they were highly favourable, but there were niggles. 'The signs are *mostly* of a promising nature,' was *Autocar*'s verdict in their 10 July 1986 issue. *Motor* (26 July) went into more detail:

> This car is not perfect, but in most major respects it surpasses the high standards laid down by its prime UK rival, the Ford Granada Scorpio. And it certainly has driver appeal and perceived quality to rival that of the German marques. Put simply, the Sterling is a very good car indeed.

It was Roger Bell in *Country Life* (17 July) who hit the nail firmly on the head when he pointed out that:

> what the 800s lack most … is head-turning presence. Alongside an SD1 Vitesse … the new cars look understated, even a bit small … the highly individualistic character has gone. Neat and clean-cut though it is, the 800 is to my eyes aesthetically undistinguished.

He was not alone in detecting that something was missing. When *Autocar* (16 July) tested a manual 825i they concluded that 'if the new Rover is lacking anything compared with its predecessors, it is perhaps character'.

The cabin earned high praise all round. 'Cabin design and decor is outstanding,' said *Country Life* (17 July). *Motor* (26 July) thought that the interior opulence would not disgrace Jaguar. However, both *Autocar* (10 July and again on 16 July) and *Motor* (26 July) commented that the sunroof ate into headroom for taller drivers. There were quibbles with detail, too. *Autocar* (16 July) and *Motor* (26 July) both found the stalk switches fiddly to use, commenting particularly on the inset thumbwheel adjusters, although the stalks themselves had a smooth action (*Autocar*, 10 July). Both also found that cabin storage space was poor. *Autocar*'s 825i manual (16 July) did not have air conditioning, and the magazine complained that the interior became stuffy without forced ventilation; *Motor*'s Sterling (26 July) did have air conditioning and occasioned no such comment.

The control layout was generally considered good. *Autocar* (10 July) praised the 'excellent, typically Japanese gearchange quality' in an 820Si, 'backed up by pedals that permit heel-and-toe downchanges, and a light clutch'. Their automatic 825i, however, would have benefited from more positive detents in the selector gate, and *Motor*'s manual Sterling (26 July) produced a noticeable 'yowl' when the clutch was depressed.

The ride 'is well up to class standards,' said *Autocar* (16 July), 'though lacking the supreme suppleness of a Jaguar'. Handling was good, too:

> Show the Rover an undulating surface and it displays exceptional damping control and large amounts of wheel travel while passengers remain in a high degree of comfort.

There was also a 'high degree of straight-line stability'. *Motor* (26 July) was less impressed, complaining that 'at low speeds it tends to over-react to transverse ridges. In extreme cases these can promote mild scuttle shake.' Overall, however, the suspension was 'excellent' and performed very well on the open road.

As for the steering, *Motor* (26 July) found that the Honda system on the V6 models was very accurate but did not have much feel. *Autocar* (16 July) agreed that there was not enough feel, but found the steering well-weighted and praised the lack of torque steer in standing-start acceleration. The British-designed PCF system on the 4-cylinder cars was generally considered to be better: *Autocar* (10 July) found it more precise, and *Country Life* (17 July) preferred it to the Honda system. The highest praise, however, was reserved for the brakes. *Autocar* had complained of some brake vibration during a spirited descent of a hill during the press launch (10 July), but described the non-ABS brakes on its 825i test car (16 July) as 'really exceptional'. *Motor* (26 July) considered them to be 'the best brakes in this class'.

The new M16 engine won a British Design Award in February 1987. Centre front right is Roland Bertodo, director of engine development for Rover, and around him are members of the engine's development team.

The overall handling was good. *Autocar* (10 July) reported first impressions of a Sterling as 'an enjoyably quick car on a fast climbing hill or a swooping descent, with typical front-drive stability which is predictable and safe, if not to be taken lightly'. On 16 July, it described its 825i test car as 'surprisingly nimble' and said that it 'feels very much a driver's car' with a 'high degree of straight-line stability'.

As for the engines, *Country Life* (17 July) found the 4-cylinders 'coarse and rather noisy'. *Autocar* (10 July) found that both 820E and 820Si models suffered from an engine vibra-

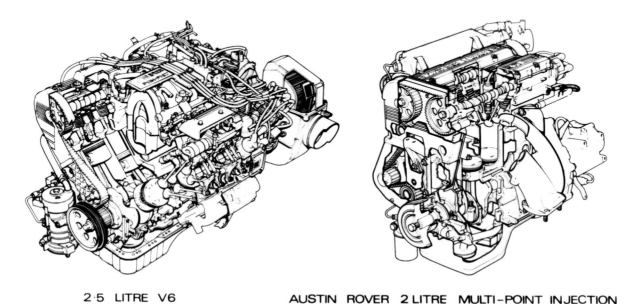

2·5 LITRE V6   AUSTIN ROVER 2 LITRE MULTI-POINT INJECTION

The two engines initially available in the 800 series were the Honda V6, seen here on the left, and the multi-point injection version of Austin Rover's own M16 4-cylinder.

tion through the steering wheel. The 820Si also droned at a cruising speed of about 50mph (80km/h); it was 'lively enough without being dramatic', and the low-speed flexibility of the lower-powered 820E was good.

However, it was quite obvious that the Honda V6 was a huge disappointment, and equally clear that the magazines were pulling punches to some extent in the way they described their reactions. The one overriding impression that it left on all the testers was that it was a very peaky engine. *Autocar* (16 July) explained:

> *The former SD1 V8 owner is going to have to get used to the idea of working the new engine very much harder than the previous torquey, all-aluminium GM-derived V8 in order to get similar levels of performance.*

TOP: **The entry-level engine, not available until some months after the launch, was the M16 with throttle-body (sometimes known as 'single-point') injection.**

MIDDLE: **This was the mid-range M16 engine with multi-point injection, used in the 820i and 820Si. The most obvious visual difference from the throttle-body injection engine was the differently shaped manifold at the back of the engine.**

BOTTOM: **The top engine for the range was the 2.5-litre Honda V6. Everything was very neatly arranged, but the engine bay appeared very full and very busy.**

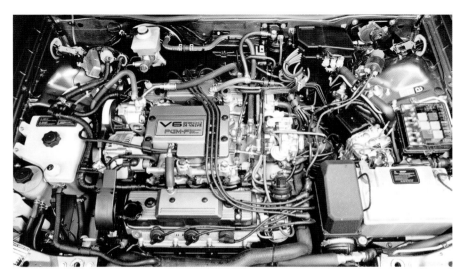

Rover were very proud of the M16 engine, and prepared a special cutaway demonstration model to show its workings. This close-up shows the combustion chamber of the throttle-body injection version.

Country Life (17 July) singled out the V6's lack of low-speed torque:

> It is ... quite tame, bereft of walloping pickup. Not until the revs reach 3,500rpm does the engine really go. Fully to exploit the manual's strong performance, you have to keep the revs up and the tallish gears low, as you would in a turbo.

Motor (26 July) complained of its 'demonstrably poor flexibility', and said it was 'just too sporting in character to suit a luxury car ... we are certain that most owners would prefer a more torquey, less frenzied, power delivery'. It was 'too lethargic in the low and mid-ranges'. They did note that it

POLICE DEMONSTRATORS

Intending to capitalize on the popularity of the SD1 model with UK police forces, Austin Rover prepared police demonstrators from early 825i models registered C472 AKV and C474 AKV.. The demonstrators did the rounds of several police forces, among the first being West Mercia, West Midlands and London's Metropolitan Police. There is more information about the 800's police career in Chapter 9.

was smooth and refined, and *Autocar*'s first impressions (10 July) had been that it was very quiet at town speeds and up to 50mph (80km/h) even though its performance was 'unexciting'. Above 4,000rpm, the engine did come alive, producing a 'surprising growl' (*Autocar*, 10 July) or a loud howl, which was either from the induction or the exhaust or both (*Autocar*, 16 July).

EARLY SALES

When Rover had introduced the SD1 model in 1976, it had been available only in its most expensive form with the 3.5-litre V8 engine, and for the best part of a year there was no official indication that 6-cylinder (2300 and 2600) models would follow. The strategy had worked: the 3500 whetted the public's appetite for the big Rover, so that the 6-cylinder cars were released onto a waiting market. (Only later would quality-control issues spoil the SD1's reputation.) It seems probable that Austin Rover's marketing people believed a similar strategy would be good for the 800 range, with the V6 models drumming up enthusiasm for the 4-cylinder cars to be released later.

This time around, however, the strategy backfired to some extent. The heavy focus on the most expensive models at the start of the 800's career had the result of making the public think that the cars were all going to be expensive. As *Motor* magazine explained in its issue dated 5 March 1988:

> Sales got off to a shaky start following AR's decision to launch the V6 models first – and with the top Sterling model priced beyond the cost of a Mercedes 300E, the entire Rover 800 range acquired an 'expensive' image. ... For several months it became a joke that the only Rover 800s seen on the roads were silver Sterlings.

So it took some time for the 4-cylinder models to make their mark when they did become available. John Parkinson, Rover Group's fleet operations director, told *Motor* for its special supplement of 24 October 1987 that:

> We simply didn't get the press coverage for the complete range. I don't know why – after all, we did launch a complete product range. People tended to pick up on the Sterling. ... The fact that our range started at under £11,000 ... seemed lost on people.

He added that when he was on the Rover Group stand at the 1986 Motor Show:

> I was amazed at the number of people who came on and said they didn't realize that the car went down to that price level. ... It appeared that even the fleet buyers weren't aware of what the 800 range actually included. Since then, we've made sure they do!

THE FIRST YEAR

Post-launch, the press releases followed thick and fast. On 11 September, Austin Rover announced that dealers would be able to apply Identicar window etching for just £20 and that the Home Office estimated having the car's registration number etched into the glass in this way reduced the rate of thefts from 1 in 50 to 1 in 2,500. A week later came a release that told of the deliberate low pricing of 100 critical parts, which it claimed would make the 800 all of 10 per cent cheaper to run than its nearest rival.

The British Motor Show in October 1986 brought the first opportunity to see cars with the lower-specification version of the M16 2-litre engine, and an 820E was displayed on the Austin Rover stand. Rover publicity used the opportunity to point out that its throttle-body injection system had been entirely designed within the company, and explained for the first time that the E in the model designations of the 820E and 820SE stood for 'electronic fuel efficiency' – which may or may not have been entirely true. Then a day after the opening of the show came the news that three major UK car rental fleets – Hertz Rent-A-Car, Godfrey Davis and Kenning Car and Van Rental – had ordered 800s, to bring in a total of £2.6 million. Of the 160 cars ordered, 140 would be 825i models and the balance would be top-model Sterlings.

News of export successes also provided valuable publicity. At the start of October came the announcement of a major expansion of Austin Rover sales in Japan, the second largest car market in the world. The new Austin Rover Japan sales company would of course be focusing its efforts on the Honda-built version of the Rover 800. Then on 12 December came the news that the first Rover 800s for the USA – wearing Sterling rather than Rover identification – would be leaving the UK a week later for a start to sales in January.

There was more positive news early in the New Year. In February, Austin Rover were able to announce that the M16

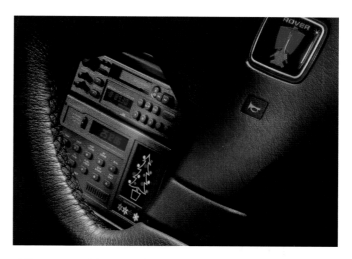

The sense of humour behind this Christmas card that Austin Rover issued to members of the motoring press was a reflection of the company's buoyant mood at Christmas 1986. The picture also helps to illustrate that the dashboard was becoming quite cluttered with its plethora of switches, buttons and controls.

Lean Burn engine had received a British Design Award. Just over a week later *What Car?* magazine gave its Best Executive Car 1987 award to the 820Si. Then at Geneva Show time in March, the news was that the catalytic converter version of the V6 engine developed for North American models would become available on European versions of the car during the second quarter of the year. This would allow sales to begin in Germany, Switzerland and Austria, so further expanding the 800's sales potential.

All car makers try to present a rosy picture of their latest products through publicity releases, so it would be wrong to suggest that Austin Rover's activity in this period was in any way unusual or unexpected. However, behind the scenes, things were not quite as rosy as they appeared. There was little doubt that the top-model 800s – fortunately, not those that were expected to be the volume-sellers in Britain – had disappointing torque characteristics. Also, there was little doubt that the sleek and svelte styling of the 800 appeared quite bland to many observers, and that the car lacked the presence of the SD1 Rover that had preceded it. And despite the determinedly British design input, the car looked strangely Japanese to some eyes!

As already noted, pricing was also an issue, and there was a degree of buyer blindness to the lower-priced models in the 800 range. In Britain, the 825i and Sterling models were

PRICE INCREASES

Austin Rover increased its UK showroom prices across the range three times during 1987. The table below shows how these changes affected the 800 Series models. Prices quoted are inclusive of taxes and have been rounded to the nearest pound.

Model	15 Oct 1986	12 Jan 1987 (+ 3.5% avge)	04 May 1987 (+ 2.4% avge)	01 Sep 1987 (+ 2.3% avge)
820E	£10,750	£10,994	£11,394	£11,925
820i	£11,820	£12,315	£12,565	£13,102
820SE	£12,391	£12,777	£12,995	£13,520
820Si	£13,247	£13,897	£14,165	£14,698
825i	£15,871	£15,995	£16,315	£16,923
Sterling	£18,795	£18,995	£19,248	£19,989

seen as expensive when compared to their SD1 predecessors and to rival models from other manufacturers. This perception was not helped when Austin Rover increased their prices – an across-the-range action not confined to the 800 Series – no fewer than three times in the first nine months of 1987. Meanwhile, the automatic option for the 820Si models had been quietly dropped for the UK market in December 1986; no reason was given.

THE 1988 MODELS

Austin Rover introduced the 1988 models at Motorfair in October 1987 but had made sure of getting some attention at the important Frankfurt Motor Show staged in early September. Here it announced a body styling kit as an optional accessory.

Body Styling Kit

The body kit had been designed by the Austin Rover design studio but its manufacture was subcontracted to TWR in Kidlington; it would not be available until later in the year. The kit consisted of a deeper front spoiler, incorporating driving lamps; an extended rear skirt with a tailpipe aperture; sill skirts similar to those shown on the CCV concept car (see Chapter 7); and a wrap-around rear deck spoiler. So when Austin Rover came to prepare its

Motorfair stand, two of the three cars on it (an 820E automatic and a Sterling) were wearing that body kit. The third car was an 820Si.

The Sterling photographed for publicity purposes with the body kit also had a feature that did not enter production: these rather attractive special wheels. The sales brochure firmly pointed out that they were not available – even though a Sterling with them on had been on the 1988 Motor Show stand.

At the start of the 1988 model year an optional body kit was introduced to add a little glamour to the 800 range. It also took some of the squareness away from the standard lines, perhaps reflecting customer feedback on the issue. The kit of sills, front and rear aprons and rear spoiler is seen here on a Sterling model, which is probably the one later registered as E348 HTH.

Minor Changes

The 1988 models brought minor changes that reflected customer feedback gathered during the first year of sales. Among these was a revision to the power steering on 4-cylinder models that gave a greater degree of 'feel'. There were three new paint colours to replace three unpopular ones, and all 800 models gained a vanity mirror with cover flap on the driver's side sun visor.

Working up from the bottom of the range, the 820E and 820i took on the wheel trims associated with the S models, and now had a revised ICE system with an auto-reverse cassette deck, loudness control and six speakers including front-door tweeters. The S-model 4-cylinders moved to 15in wheels with 195/65 VR 15 tyres and gained burr walnut inserts in their door trims. They also had a better-quality ICE system, now with Dolby sound, adaptability for chrome or metal tapes (these were more durable than earlier varieties but wore the tape heads more quickly), and a track search function. There were separate bass and treble controls, and the head unit's output increased to 4 x 7 watts, while there were now eight instead of six speakers with a higher power handling capability.

There were fewer changes for the two V6 models. The 1988-model 825i gained electric operation for its sunroof and the same eight-speaker ICE system as the S models. The Sterling took on cruise control and the scope of the two-tone option was also widened: the Gunmetal lower panels were now available with eleven of the twelve colours, the exception being Black.

THE REALITY OF OWNERSHIP

Both of the leading British weekly motoring magazines, *Autocar* and *Motor*, took early examples of the 800 range onto their long-term test fleets. *Autocar* had an 820SE with manual gearbox, and *Motor* an 820i, also with manual gearbox. Both had a number of problems with their cars, and reports in the magazines were worrying enough to have deterred some would-be buyers.

Bought in February 1987, *Motor*'s 820i provided some interesting insight into ownership of an early Rover 800 during this period. In December 1987, it was recalled for an ignition switch problem that could cause complete electrical failure while the car was in motion. The ignition switch was changed – but not until February 1988 because the new part was not available. Over its first few thousand miles it also suffered from an 'occasional engine hiccup when indicating right turn', which was finally cured by replacing the engine's electronic control unit (ECU). Both of these potentially dangerous faults should surely never have been allowed to escape Rover's quality-control system.

In the magazine's issue dated 5 March 1988, two further faults were reported. One was an intermittent misfire above 4,000rpm, and the other a speedometer that was seriously under-reading, showing 55mph when the car was travelling at 80mph. The engine then developed a tendency to stall for no obvious reason; the magazine reported

in its 28 May 1988 issue that this was traced to a potentiometer fault, 'the electrics telling the engine to idle at impossibly low revs'. It was eventually sorted out satisfactorily, but not before the driver had suffered a near-miss with a brick wall when the engine had cut out in a corner taken at low speed.

The *Autocar* 820SE led its user, Martin Lewis, a merry dance. In the 3 February 1988 issue he wrote:

> It has been like living through a twelve-month long episode of Tales of the Unexpected. I have never been quite certain of just what the 820SE would – or would not – do next.

PAINT AND TRIM OPTIONS – 1987–1988 MODELS

1987 model year

There were twelve paint options, of which four were solid colours and the other eight were clearcoat metallic. Sterling models could be ordered with two-tone paintwork (usually called 'Duo Tone' paintwork in sales literature), featuring Gunmetal lower panels with Oporto Red, Shantung Gold, Silver Leaf or White Diamond upper panels.

There were four interior colours: Coffee Beige, Flint, Mink and Prussian Blue. Entry-level upholstery (820E and 820i) was in Plain Velvet; there was Chalkstripe and Plain Velvet for the 820SE and 820Si models; the 825i had Diagonal and Plain Velvet, or leather at extra cost; and the Sterling had leather as standard but could have Diagonal and Plain Velvet as a no-cost option.

The options were:

Paint	Interior
Azure Blue (metallic)	Flint or Prussian Blue
Black	Coffee Beige or Flint
Burgundy Red	Coffee Beige or Mink
Lynx Bronze (metallic)	Coffee Beige or Mink
Moonraker Blue (metallic)	Flint or Prussian Blue
Oporto Red (metallic)	Coffee Beige or Mink
Shantung Gold (metallic)	Coffee Beige or Flint
Silk Green (metallic)	Flint
Silver Leaf (metallic)	Flint or Prussian Blue
Strata Grey (metallic)	Flint or Mink
Targa Red	Coffee Beige or Flint
White Diamond	Coffee Beige or Flint

1988 model year

There were again twelve paint options, of which three were new. Atlantic Blue, Pulsar Silver and Stone Grey replaced Moonraker Blue, Oporto Red and Silk Green. Sterling models could be ordered with all colours except for Black, and came with Duo Tone paintwork, featuring Gunmetal lower panels.

The same four interior colours were available. Entry-level upholstery (820E and 820i) was in Plain Velvet; there was Chalkstripe and Plain Velvet for the 820SE and 820Si models; the 825i had Diagonal and Plain Velvet, or leather at extra cost; and the Sterling had leather as standard but could have Diagonal and Plain Velvet as a no-cost option.

The options were:

Paint	Interior
Atlantic Blue	Flint or Prussian Blue
Azure Blue (metallic)	Flint or Prussian Blue
Black	Coffee Beige or Flint
Burgundy Red	Coffee Beige or Mink
Lynx Bronze (metallic)	Coffee Beige or Mink
Pulsar Silver	Flint or Mink
Shantung Gold (metallic)	Coffee Beige or Flint
Silver Leaf (metallic)	Flint or Prussian Blue
Stone Grey	Coffee Beige, Flint
Strata Grey (metallic)	Flint or Mink
Targa Red	Coffee Beige or Flint
White Diamond	Coffee Beige or Flint

TECHNICAL SPECIFICATIONS – 1987–1988 MODELS

Engines

M16e and M16i 4-cylinder petrol

Iron block with aluminium alloy cylinder head

1994cc (84.5 x 89mm)

Twin ohc, belt-driven

4v per cylinder

Five-bearing crankshaft

Compression ratio 10.0:1

M16e

ARG throttle-body injection

120PS (118bhp) at 5,600rpm

162Nm (119lb ft) at 3,500rpm

M16i

Lucas multi-point injection

140PS (138bhp) at 6,000rpm

178Nm (131lb ft) at 4,500rpm

Honda C25A V6 petrol

Aluminium alloy block and cylinder head

2494cc (84 x 75mm)

Single ohc on each cylinder bank

4v per cylinder

Five-bearing crankshaft

Compression ratio 9.6:1

Honda PGM-FI multi-point injection

173PS (171bhp) at 6,000rpm with manual gearbox; 167PS (165bhp) at 6,000rpm with automatic gearbox

217Nm (160lb ft) at 5,000rpm with manual gearbox; 221Nm (163lb ft) at 4,000rpm with automatic gearbox

Transmission

Five-speed manual gearbox standard
(4-cylinder models; Honda type PG1 G6)
Ratios 3.25:1, 1.89:1, 1.31:1, 1.03:1, 0.85:1; reverse 3.00:1
(V6 models; Honda type PG2)
Ratios 2.92:1, 1.79:1, 1.22:1, 0.91:1, 0.72:1; reverse 3.00:1

Four-speed automatic gearbox optional
(4-cylinder models; ZF type 4HP 14)
Ratios 2.41:1, 1.37:1, 1.00:1, 0.74:1; reverse 2.83:1
(V6 models; Honda type EAT)
Ratios 2.65:1, 1.46:1, 0.97:1, 0.68:1; reverse 1.90:1

Axle ratio

3.94:1   4-cylinder models with manual gearbox

4.20:1   All V6 models

4.40:1   4-cylinder models with automatic gearbox

Suspension, steering and brakes

Front suspension with unequal length double wishbones, steel coil springs and elastomeric compound spring aids, co-axial telescopic dampers and anti-roll bar

Rear suspension with independent struts, transverse and trailing links, steel coil springs and elastomeric compound spring aids, telescopic dampers and anti-roll bar. Boge Nivomat self-levelling dampers on V6 models only

Rack-and-pinion steering with power assistance as standard: TRW Cam Gears type PCF on 4-cylinder models; Honda speed proportional type on V6 models

Disc brakes all round, with single-cylinder floating calipers; handbrake acting on rear discs

Ventilated front discs with 262mm diameter on 4-cylinder models and 285mm diameter on V6 models

Solid rear discs with 260mm diameter on all models

Two diagonally split hydraulic circuits; ABS optional on 825i and standard on Sterling

Dimensions

Overall length	184.8in (4,694mm)	
Overall width	68.1in (1,730mm)	
	76.6in (1,946mm) over mirrors	
Overall height	55in (1,398mm)	
Wheelbase	108.6in (2,759mm)	
Front track	58.7in (1,492mm)	
Rear track	57.1in (1,450mm)	

Wheels and tyres

6J x 14 steel wheels with 195/70 HR 14 tyres on 4-cylinder models

6J x 15 alloy wheels with 195/65 VR 15 tyres on V6 models

Kerb weight

2,800lb (1,270kg)	820i manual
2,844lb (1,290kg)	820i automatic
2,855lb (1,295kg)	820Si manual
2,899lb (1,315kg)	820Si automatic
2,998lb (1,360kg)	825i manual
3,042lb (1,380kg)	825i automatic
3,086lb (1,400kg)	Sterling manual
3,131lb (1,420kg)	Sterling automatic

Lewis had plenty to say in the car's defence:

When behaving, it has been a car which is a delight to drive, equally at home in bumper-to-bumper city traffic or cruising at over 100mph on West German Autobahnen. It is quiet, very comfortable and reasonably quick – but how I wish it had been able to remain working for rather longer between scheduled service intervals.

The list of failings was nevertheless quite frightening, and would have left a lasting impression on anybody who had read it. It made quite clear that quality control was not yet good enough on the 800 assembly lines at Rover's Cowley factory.

Twice in the past year, the car has been left for dead, victim of malfunctions in its starter circuit. The heater and ventilator controls have minds of their own, repeatedly working loose or falling off. Twice the electric window in the driver's door has packed up, thankfully with it closed. And in December, the car was recalled so that a possible fault in the ignition switch could be investigated. [This was the same recall that affected the Autocar 820i.]

PERFORMANCE AND FUEL CONSUMPTION FIGURES – 1987–1988 MODELS

These figures are the ones claimed by the manufacturer.

	0–60mph	Maximum speed	Fuel consumption
820E manual	10.5sec	119mph (192km/h)	34.6mpg
820E automatic	11.9sec	117mph (188km/h)	34.6mpg
820i/820Si manual	8.8sec	126mph (203km/h)	33.9mpg (8.3ltr/100km)
825i/Sterling manual	7.8sec	133mph (214km/h)	29.7mpg (9.5ltr/100km)
825i/Sterling automatic	9.0sec	131mph (211km/h)	28.4mpg (10ltr/100km)

CHAPTER THREE

THE 2.7 AND FASTBACK, 1988–1989

The second stage of the 800's production story did not arrive at a single stroke. It was phased in over a period of three months in the first half of 1988. First came an improved – 2.7-litre – version of the Honda engine that led to name changes for the V6-engined 800s. Then came a new hatchback body style, sold alongside the existing saloon and known by its marketing name of Fastback.

However, global sales had already begun to slide, just eighteen months into the car's production life. The production figures for the 1987 calendar year were the best the 800 range would ever achieve at 54,434, a figure that was buoyed by some 14,000 cars for the USA (see Chapter 5). The US market rapidly became disenchanted with the 800, and by the end of 1988 the car's transatlantic sales had virtually collapsed. Sadly, not even the improved new models delivered by the Rover Group over the next three years were able to reverse what had become a global trend. The 800 had already become a disappointment to its manufacturers.

THE 2.7-LITRE V6 AND THE EAT

The main failing of the original 2.5-litre Honda V6 engine was that it lacked torque at low crankshaft speeds. This was largely masked when it was allied to an automatic gearbox, but it was sufficiently marked in manual-gearbox cars to provoke some negative customer feedback. Austin Rover had been aware of this shortcoming from the start but had hoped that their own V6 engine would be available early enough to counter it. However, this would be some time in coming, so the British company had no option but to put pressure on their Japanese colleagues for a version of the engine that would have better torque characteristics.

Honda appreciated the problem and delivered a new big-bore version of the engine with a 2.7-litre swept volume, which they went on to use in their own versions of the

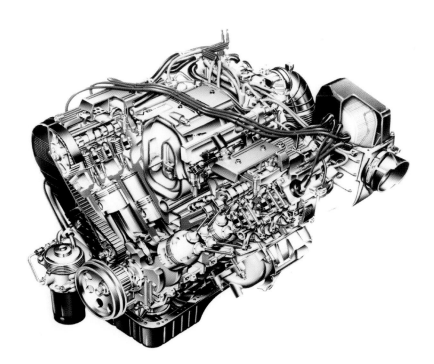

The larger-bore 2.7-litre Honda V6 benefited from a new variable-length intake system, which improved torque. This cutaway diagram was issued to the media in February 1988.

ABOVE: **The new 2.7-litre engine looked essentially the same as the older 2.5-litre type under the bonnet, but it carried '2700' identification.**

LEFT: **The new 2.7-litre engine made the V6 models much better cars to drive.**

car. However, the larger capacity was not the key feature of Honda's C27A engine. What really made the difference was a variable-length inlet manifold. Power remained much the same as before, with 177PS (175bhp) at 6,000rpm, but torque improved to 228Nm (168lb ft) at 4,500rpm (Austin Rover had begun to use German power and torque measurements). The wider torque band that came with it allowed better acceleration both in and through the gears in the 800.

The 827SLi, 827Si and 827 Sterling

The new engine became available in February 1988, replacing the earlier 2.5-litre V6. It went into the top-of-the-range Sterling models and into the 827SLi model, a direct replacement for the old 825i. It also went into a new V6 model, the 827Si. Priced below the 827SLi, this carried a level of trim and equipment equivalent to the 4-cylinder S models. The 827SLi retained the bright grille bar of the old 825i and

its high equipment level, while the new 827 Sterling was distinguished by the cross-spoke alloy wheels that had been pioneered on the US-model Sterling (*see* Chapter 5).

Rover's photographer finally managed to get a good black-and-white shot of the Sterling, which for 1988 came with a new design of alloy wheel.

The 827SLi delivered a new trim level just below the Sterling. As seen here, it came with steel wheels and appropriate badging on the tail.

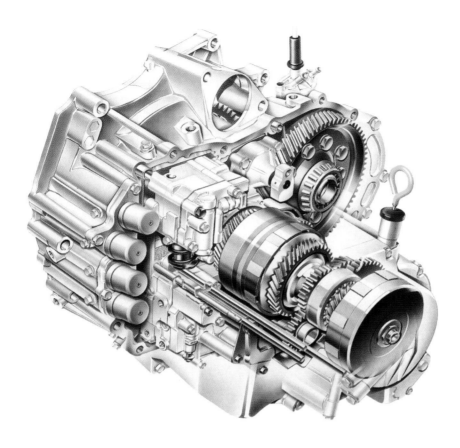

On the 2.7-litre cars, Honda's four-speed automatic gearbox came with an electronic control system.

(for Sport) setting. This allowed the gearbox to hold on to the immediate gears for longer and prevented it from changing into top gear. Pressing a button labelled S4 alongside the selector would then allow the gearbox to change into top gear. The arrangement was slightly odd, but worked well enough once the driver was used to it.

There were some interior changes too. The Sterling models took on a new centre console with a raised and colour-keyed driver's armrest. The electric seat controls and the switches for the seat heaters and sunroof were all changed, and with the new automatic gearbox came a new selector gate, set in a burr walnut panel. All 800 models now came with two keys: a master that operated everything and another for just the doors and ignition. The new system allowed valuables to be left locked safely in the boot or the glovebox when the car was lent out or valet parked.

The Sterling also gained ABS as standard, at this stage the only model in the range to do so. Other models could be fitted with ABS at extra cost, but in practice the option remained rare. Anti-theft equipment was also still an extra-cost option.

Other Changes

New also in February 1988 was a four-speed automatic gearbox with electronic control, sometimes known as the EAT (Electronic Automatic Transmission). This was made standard on all the V6 models, although they could be ordered with a manual gearbox for no extra cost. The manual gearbox, the Honda-built PG2 type, was modified at the same time, taking on lower third, fourth and fifth gear ratios to improve acceleration at higher speeds. The 4-cylinder models retained their existing ZF automatic option.

The electronic control system of the EAT gave it two key features: a progressive torque converter lock-up in second, third and fourth gears, and dual-mode operation. The lock-up feature improved overrun engine braking and made a contribution towards better fuel economy. The dual-mode feature came with a selector gate that incorporated an S

Seen here on an 827SLi, although not unique to the model, are the redesigned console and gear shift for the 1988 season.

The electric seat adjustment controls were also redesigned for 1988. By more recent standards, the profusion of buttons appears confusing.

THE 827 MODELS AND THE PRESS

The new 2.7-litre engine certainly went down well. Press demonstrators were 827SLi models rather than top-model Sterlings, and both *Autocar* (2 March 1988) and *Motor* (5 March 1988) published detailed road tests. *Autocar*'s example had automatic transmission, which was expected to prove the popular choice, while *Motor*'s example had a manual gearbox.

Autocar wrote:

> Two years on from the launch of the Rover 800, the 6-cylinder cars have the engine they always needed. … The bigger engine, lower gearing and new gearbox have made the Rover 827 a real performance saloon.

Motor noted that:

> The good news is that the improvements are notice-able in ordinary motoring. The 827 cuts its predecessor's through-the-gears 30 to 70mph 'overtaking time' from 8.2sec to a considerably more lithe 7.4sec. … Some V6 gruffness remains as you approach the heady 6,400rpm rev limit, but this is not a serious criticism now that the engine works so well lower down the scale; generally, smoothness and refine-ment are of a very high order.

Performance was noticeably improved when compared with the earlier 2.5-litre engine. *Autocar* returned a maximum speed of 131mph (211km/h) as against the earlier car's 125mph (201km/h) on test, and a 0–60mph accelera-tion time of 8.4sec as compared with the earlier model's 10.1sec. The manual car tried by *Motor* recorded a maximum speed of 136.6mph (220km/h), compared with their 2.5-litre figure of 130.2mph (209km/h), and 0–60mph in a very quick 7.8sec.

Motor found the manual gearbox impressive:

> Enthusiasts would do well to consider the delete-option manual transmission. The shift is quick and positive, and complemented by perfectly stepped ratios. By large-car standards, this is a particularly fine gearbox – far superior to the manual transmis-sions available on Ford and Vauxhall rivals.

'The ride is still one of its strong points,' thought *Autocar*. 'It doesn't have the benchmark suppleness of an XJ6 but it's at least the equal of its German rivals.' *Motor* nevertheless complained that 'very severe bumps can cause the suspen-sion to bottom-out abruptly'. *Autocar* went on to praise the brakes, saying that they were 'first class [and] provide pro-gressive and powerful retardation up to a maximum of 1.1g before the optional anti-lock comes into effect'. The same magazine went on to praise both the handling and the steer-ing at length:

The Rover has plenty of grip and can be hustled around with an agility that seems at odds with its size and 1,400kg kerb weight. Pushed hard it can be made to understeer markedly, but lift off the throttle in a bend and there's not a trace of oversteer.

Honda's speed sensitive steering gives the Rover good feel and excellent stability at high speed yet it is much lighter at low speeds – perhaps, we suspect, too light for some tastes. It can still appear to be confused about the level of power assistance that is required when the Rover is slowed rapidly from speed – the steering remaining heavy until the system has had time to catch up.

Overall, *Motor* was very impressed:

There's no doubt that the Rover 827 is a very accomplished mainstream executive car. . . . Fitted with the five-speed manual gearbox, the 827 is really competing in a more sporting arena … [and it] may be seen as a viable alternative to the departing BMW 528i, or a Lancia Thema Turbo.

We have no hesitation in recommending it; the car is comfortable, refined and undeniably luxurious, while its new engine performs well enough to complement an acknowledged fine chassis; it drives well, it's tolerably economical [the car returned an overall 23.3mpg (12.1ltr/100km) on test] and it is superbly built.

Nevertheless, that superb build quality was still not universal. Although *Motor* was 'particularly impressed with the improved wind sealing compared with earlier examples', *Autocar* came away with a very different impression:

What lets the Rover 827 down is its unacceptably high level of wind noise. This may be down to build quality – the driver's door on our test car required a good slam to close it properly – but for £17,878 you have a right to expect better.

The magazine concluded that 'Austin Rover still needs to look hard at its quality control if it expects to compete on equal terms with its rivals.' Quite clearly, the manufacturing lessons that Rover had hoped to learn from its Japanese partner had not been universally applied.

THE NEW FASTBACKS, MAY 1988

During the design stages of XX, Rover and Honda had acknowledged each other's right to take the XX design forward in whatever way they saw fit once the Legend and 800 models had entered production. Rover were particularly keen to develop a hatchback derivative that would pick up where their own SD1 had left off, but Honda had no interest in such a model. Their target market was the USA, where a big hatchback was more or less an unknown quantity. Rover's target, by contrast, was Europe, where the SD1 had attracted a strong customer following and the latest Ford Granada's hatchback configuration was a tacit acknowledgement of the trend.

Roy Axe's design studio had designed the 800 saloon with one eye on a future hatchback derivative; the rear doors, for example, were planned to suit the lines of such a model without change. So when they turned to the design of the planned hatchback, they were able to retain the main structure of the car more or less unchanged. The rear end was redrawn to incorporate a hatchback, and it appears that the angle of the tailgate was identical to that of the SD1. New monosides were needed, plus a new roof panel and the tailgate itself. Minor associated panels apart, that was all, which was a real triumph of design planning.

The next stage was to pitch the hatchback version of the XX into the market in the right way. It was not a simple SD1 replacement, because this car would be sold alongside the three-box saloon derivative, and it would be important to differentiate the two quite clearly. An early plan had been to call the hatchback a Rover 600, which would have restricted both price and model range too much by making it deliberately downmarket of the 800 saloons. So this plan was abandoned – and the Rover 600 that appeared in 1993 was a totally separate model.

To get a feel for public expectations, during 1987 Rover Group ran a programme of customer clinics. From these they learned that three-box saloon models were perceived as classic, elegant and well-appointed cars, while hatchbacks were perceived as more sporty and more dynamic. This set of perceptions even seems to have fed into the naming of the car. 'Hatchback' may have been the generic term, but the word suggested small family cars rather than executive-class models like the 800. So the new model was christened the 'Fastback', a name that suggested a more sporty orientation.

This was a styling model for the Vitesse, dating probably from 1987. The car has the US-pattern Sterling wheels in their Rover-badged form, and the side bump-strips are colour-coded. Neither would be a feature of the production models. The front number plate reads, 'XX Vitesse'.

It also played well with a growing demand for sporty executive cars in Europe.

The marketing plan envisaged Fastback derivatives as direct equivalents of the entry-level and mid-range Rover 800s, but it also made some clear distinctions at the top and bottom ends of the range. There would be a new entry-level car, a Fastback priced below the cheapest of the saloons, and, at the top end of the range, there would be no Fastback equivalent of the Sterling. Instead, there would be a performance-oriented derivative that would take on the Vitesse name that had been used for the high-performance versions of the SD1.

The marketing plan had been translated into a clear pricing hierarchy for the new fourteen-model UK 800 range by the time the Fastback models were launched on 25 May 1988. It was still the

The new Fastback models arrived late in the 1988 season but few are likely to have been delivered before the 1989 model year opened in the autumn. The new Fastbacks seen here were photographed for the launch publicity, with the sporting Vitesse variant in the foreground.

The clean lines of the **XX** suited the Fastback model very well. As seen here, the Vitesse had a distinguishing tail spoiler and five-spoke alloy wheels.

RIGHT: **At the other end of the Fastback range from the Vitesse was the new 820 model, which featured a lower-powered 2-litre engine and was priced as the entry-level model to the 800 range.**

Rover had done very well in the large executive-car class with the hatchback SD1 and they had no intention of losing the advantage of such a model. This is the 820 version again.

The Fastback offered a large and versatile loadspace. The rear seat folded forwards to increase the length available ...

... and this shot from inside the car makes clear just how long that loadspace could become.

1988 model year, but in practice these were 1989 models – none were available for European markets until September 1988, when the 1989 model year began.

The seven-model Fastback range for the UK duly emerged as beginning with an 820 model, which came with an engine new to the range. It then went on up through 820e, 820Se, 820i, 820Si and 827Si to end with the Vitesse; the two models with throttle-body injection were now known as 820e and 820Se (with a lower-case 'e'), and both carried new badges reflecting that. The mechanical specification and equipment levels of the mid-range models deliberately paralleled those of the similarly named saloon variants, but the 820 and Vitesse had unique specifications. All Fastback models came with an electric tailgate release beside the driver's seat (an idea borrowed from Honda), a removable rear parcel shelf and a rear seat that folded forwards to make a roomy load area. The Fastbacks also had an additional front bib spoiler and claret inserts in their side bump-strip mouldings, two features that helped to make them what the press release called 'distinctively styled sporty cars'.

When the Fastbacks arrived in May 1988, rear badges of the M16e-engined models changed to feature a lower-case 'e'.

The 820 Fastback

Its attractive new price aside, what made the 820 interesting was its engine. This was a 100PS (99bhp) version of the 2-valve 4-cylinder engine that had sired the M16 4-valve engine in the models higher up the range. Somewhat surprisingly for 1988, it came with an electronically controlled

SU HIF44 carburettor rather than fuel injection. However, it was not quite like the old O-series as its water pump was now driven by the timing belt – in fact, Rover service literature usually refers to it as an M8 type (an M-series engine with 8v rather than the 16v of the M16).

This lower-specification engine helped to keep the showroom price down and made a clear distinction between the 820 Fastback and the next model up the range, the 820e. The 820 was no ball of fire. It took 11.6sec to reach 60mph from rest in its usual manual-gearbox form, and even longer when fitted with the optional automatic. It also had steel wheels with rather dowdy plastic trims and 175 HR 14 tyres – smaller than on any other 800 derivative. Clearly, this was a car for fleet users and those who wanted the comfort of the Rover 800 but were content to settle for only average performance.

The Vitesse

At the top end of the Fastback range, the Vitesse had been designed as a sporty performance car. A UK TV advertisement, complete with German-language elements, confidently promoted it as a rival for Audi, BMW and Mercedes saloons, but its appearance and specification were something of a disappointment. Its V6 engine had the same 177PS (175bhp) tune as the other 6-cylinder 800s, and although standardization of the manual gearbox allowed it to be driven with a degree of vigour, it could also be had with the automatic, which was more commonly found with the V6 engine. Its top speed of 140mph (225km/h) made it 'the fastest Rover ever', according to the launch press release. The extra couple of miles per hour over the other V6 models was supposedly made possible by the standard body kit of front and rear spoilers and sculpted sills. These aerodynamic addenda gave the Vitesse a drag coefficient of 0.30 as against the 0.32 of other Fastback 800s.

While other Fastbacks had a black bib spoiler at the front, that on the Vitesse was painted to match the main apron spoiler. It also came with all-black side rubbing-strips and bumper inserts. The Vitesse was further distinguished by a windscreen shade band and by five-spoke alloy wheels not available on other 800s, although these were somehow too svelte for a car of its pretensions. Just four body colours were available at launch, and all were matched by a special interior that invariably came in Flint. Described as a 'designer Jacquard fabric', the upholstery incorporated a lightning-flash pattern, and both front seats carried Vitesse labels. The driver's seat

---

MORE PRICE INCREASES

Price increases were becoming a way of life for Austin Rover in the later 1980s, and there were two more in the first half of 1988. The fourth column in the table below shows the introductory prices of the new 2.7-litre models in February 1988. Saloon and Fastback models with the same designation cost the same; the 827SLi and Sterling came only as saloons; and the Vitesse only as a Fastback. Prices quoted are inclusive of taxes; automatic transmission cost £698 extra on all models.

Model		11 Jan 1988 (+ 3% average)	16 Feb 1988 (new models)	16 May 1988 (+ 2.5% average)
820	Fastback			£11,995
820E	Saloon/Fastback	£12,489		£12,851
820i	Saloon/Fastback	£13,678		£14,090
820SE	Saloon/Fastback	£13,912		£14,178
820Si	Saloon/Fastback	£15,102		£15,417
827Si	Saloon/Fastback		£16,550	£16,947
825i	Saloon	£17,431		
827SLi	Saloon		£17,878	£18,307
Vitesse	Fastback			£19,944
Sterling (2.5)	Saloon	£20,733		
Sterling (2.7)	Saloon		£21,380	£21,893

came with electric height adjustment and adjustable lumbar support as standard. A leather-trimmed steering wheel and trip computer were standard, as were burr walnut on the centre console, reading lamps and a cigarette lighter in the rear, and an electric tilt-and-slide sunroof.

What really lived up to expectations of the Vitesse name, however, was the specially developed suspension package. Those five-spoke alloy wheels carried 205/60 VR 15 tyres, wider and with a lower profile than on any other 800. There were stiffer anti-roll bars and gas-pressurized dampers, and the whole sports suspension package was claimed to increase the roll stiffness at the front by 22 per cent and at the rear by a massive 118 per cent. It was perhaps no sur-

prise that this suspension package was also made available at extra cost on the Fastback versions of the 820Si and 827Si. In keeping with the performance image of the car, ABS was standard equipment.

CROSS-RANGE CHANGES, MAY 1988

Rover used the opportunity of the Fastback launch to make some specification changes right across the 800 range. All the M16-engined cars gained revised gearing, which improved their acceleration from rest and reduced engine

Though devoid of many of the features associated with its more expensive cousins, the 820 Fastback was by no means spartan inside.

The Vitesse came with a new 'lightning' fabric upholstery intended to give a more sporty feel to the passenger cabin.

This was the interior of an 820e, in this case with automatic transmission.

The interior of the S-level models was again different. This one has a manual gearbox.

Leather and additional wood trim made the interior of the Sterling appear more inviting. This style of centre console, with revised selector lever, was initially available only on the Sterling.

revs at speed to improve fuel economy and refinement. Second-generation Bosch ABS, already standard on the Sterling, became optional on all the 2-litre models for the first time. The Boge Nivomat self-levelling system was also optional for all models – except for the 820 (designed as a bargain-basement model) and the Vitesse (where it was incompatible with the sports suspension).

On the inside, the 820e and 820i models took on new injection-moulded door casings with a new design of interior release and different locations for the door pulls and speakers. On the S models and the Vitesse, a new release handle and escutcheon were added to the existing S-type casings, and both cars came with electrically adjusted and heated door mirrors. Electric window switches, where fitted, were now relocated on the centre console. Finally, all models gained improved theft resistance for the doors and bonnet, and the anti-theft alarm system now became an extra-cost option across the whole range.

THE FASTBACK MODELS AND THE PRESS

When the Fastback models arrived in the early summer of 1988, they were of course subjected to scrutiny in the motoring press. In its issue of 28 May 1988, *Motor* compared an 820Si against three of its rivals – a Ford Granada 2.0i Ghia, a Fiat Croma SX and a Renault 25TX – and reported that the Rover had been the testers' favourite. Although the ride was 'too firm and taut to be considered really comfortable', the car:

> *performs well, has safe competent handling, good brakes and a slick set of controls. The 'fastback' styling not only looks good but offers reasonable load-carrying practicality and the car has the most inviting and expensively trimmed interior. In the light of these virtues, we'd forgive it for not having the roomiest interior or the smoothest ride.*

The primary interest, though, was in the new Vitesse Fastback, and both *Autocar* and *Motor* reserved many of their comments about the new five-door configuration for their reports on that car. Once again, *Autocar* took a test car with an automatic gearbox, while *Motor* had one with the manual gearbox, which seemed to be more appropriate for a car that Rover advertisements described as the fastest production Rover ever. In practice, both magazines were disappointed with the car, and the *Autocar* report of 25 May 1988 was quite damning. It concluded:

It's when you start searching for evidence of Vitesse charisma and ability that you are disappointed. … You are left with an expensive car with a tail spoiler and the hollow promise of the Vitesse badges. It is patently not enough.

More specifically:

Rover claimed a faster 0–60 time for the old Vitesse than it does for the new one – 7.1sec against 7.6 in manual form – which suggests that a certain amount of licence is being used in the 'fastest Rover ever' claim. Certainly in automatic form no such claim is justified.

The magazine went on to complain that:

this supposedly sporting car is a second and a half slower to 60 than the equivalently engined Rover 827SLi saloon automatic … and for that there can be no excuse. At most the Fastback tips the scales at 50lb more than the equivalent saloon.

Nor did the test car live up to Rover's claim of 8.5sec for the 0–60mph sprint; *Autocar* managed only 9.7sec, which it described as 'not unacceptable even though we, and Rover, expected a lot better'.

There was worse to come:

Handling overrides the missing performance as the Vitesse's major disappointment. Again, the Vitesse name promises more than the car delivers; indeed we are not sure this car has as much front end grip as lesser 800s, despite the promise of uprated suspension and wider, lower profile tyres. … For a car aimed at enthusiastic drivers, the steering too is inappropriate … too light at low speed and too lacking in feedback when pressing on.

The Fastback configuration had some merits, but was not flawless, either:

*There can be no denying the Fastback's extra luggage practicality, even though in some ways it's plain that this is not a purpose-designed load carrier … [*Autocar* found it too narrow between the rear strut turrets] … The provision of a split folding rear seat,*

or even a cubbyhole for fishing rods or skis in the rear backrest, would go a long way to making up for this [and] we feel this is a significant omission.

Motor was more impressed with the manual Vitesse in its 2 July 1988 issue, although once again performance no better than that of other 2.7-litre V6 Rovers deserved comment:

The Vitesse is the best Rover 800 both visually and dynamically. The promise of its handsomely aggressive looks is fulfilled by the V6 engine coupled with delicate suspension modifications. … Its responses are crisp and fluid, its ride only slightly impaired. … The performance figures are a slight disappointment but the superb Honda V6 does much to sweeten the pill.

Although the Vitesse was potentially a 140mph car, 'so is the 827SLi tested recently'. On the banked track at MIRA, *Motor* was unable to reach the claimed top speed because of tyre scrub, but 'on a level Autobahn the Vitesse will hit the magic figure, its aerodynamic addenda just managing to overcome the extra drag created by its wider tyres'.

Motor liked the 'slick, five-speed gearbox with well-judged ratios' and found that 'the steering seems more positive, giving sharper turn-in and the grip generated by its wide Dunlops is tremendous. On smooth tarmac the car simply dives into a corner and goes round, such is its poise.'

At the other end of the range, *Motor* tried an 820 Fastback in its issue dated 6 August 1988. They found this:

a curious machine conceptually in that it seems to be an almost retrograde step in the high-tech Honda/ARG collaboration; an O-series 98bhp 820 is much less powerful than any of the obvious opposition now on sale in the UK. … ARG must be hoping that a market for it exists among drivers who are not interested in cut and thrust on the open road, but like to savour their creature comforts driving at a more leisurely pace.

The car had all the strengths of other 800 models, and its build quality and finish were especially good. Economy, at 27.6mpg (10.3ltr/100km) overall, was also good as long as the driver did not thrash the car to compensate for the lack of power. Refinement was up to the usual 800 Series standards: 'In most everyday situations … the O-series engine remains

CORPORATE CHANGES AT ROVER

The Rover 800 was born into a time of corporate upheaval for its manufacturers. Austin Rover was still an element in the British Leyland empire that had been nationalized by the British Government in 1975, and was therefore still costing the taxpayer money. After ten years, the government was keen to see British Leyland privatized, and plans were set in motion.

There were talks with Ford about buying the car business, and similar talks with General Motors about buying the truck and bus business, which included Land Rover. However, both sets of talks failed. Prime Minister Margaret Thatcher was nevertheless determined to press ahead and make the main element in the British motor industry stand on its own two feet. In 1986, she appointed a Canadian businessman, Graham Day, to the position of BL's chairman and managing director. Shortly after that, the remains of British Leyland were renamed the Rover Group plc. The Rover name was supposedly chosen because it was the only one of the marque names available to the group that still had a degree of public respect.

Over the next couple of years, the business was slimmed down. In 1987, the Leyland Trucks division (which by then included the Freight Rover van division) merged with DAF. The Unipart spare parts division was sold to its management later that year. The Leyland Bus division followed, and went to Volvo Buses in 1988. In the meantime, the design and engineering functions of the Rover car and Land Rover business were brought together – in an effort, one senior insider told the author, to make it impossible for any eventual purchaser to split them apart and resell them separately. 'It was an entirely political move,' he claimed.

A purchaser was eventually found in 1988, and the Rover Group was sold to British Aerospace for £150 million. This derisory sum caused outrage at the headquarters of the European Union in Brussels, and a later evaluation of the Rover Group's true worth (carried out, somewhat ironically, by Ford) set its value at £800 million.

Meanwhile, British Aerospace retained Graham Day as joint CEO and chairman of the Rover Group, and appointed Kevin Morley as managing director of Rover Cars. Morley had earlier been the company's sales director. In 1989, there was a further change of name, to Rover Group Holdings Ltd.

AN 800 JOINS THE ROYAL NAVY

On 13 June 1988, an Atlantic Blue Rover Sterling was handed over to the captain of the aircraft carrier HMS *Ark Royal* for official duties. The car was used for shore duties during a six-month mission called Outback '88, when the carrier and other Royal Navy ships promoted British interests by mounting a series of exhibitions of sea and air power in the Far East.

A Rover Sterling was presented to the aircraft carrier HMS *Ark Royal* for official duties during June 1988. The car carried the ship's emblem on its front doors and a customized number plate. Captain Mike Harris is pictured here receiving the keys from Rover's international operations director, Brian Fuller.

THE FASTBACK BODY KIT

A body kit for the Fastback versions of the 800 became available at the start of June 1988 through Rover Group dealers. It cost £1,675 fitted, but the version for the Vitesse was cheaper at £1,475 because that model already had a rear spoiler as standard. A feature of this kit was stainless-steel exhaust tips.

pleasantly muted, but [if rapid acceleration is needed] a gruff straining of the engine will tell you that this is no performance machine.' On the whole, the 820 Fastback was a good car, but 'on those rare occasions when an open road beckons, this Rover is disadvantaged by a sheer lack of brake horse power'.

THE 1989 MODEL YEAR

Between them, the new Fastbacks and the accompanying changes to other Rover models had already previewed the 1989 models by the time of the Motor Show in October 1988. However, Rover Group did capitalize on a number of further changes that built on those already announced.

The centrepiece of the Rover stand at the Birmingham NEC was a sectioned 800, split behind the rear doors to display the alternative options of Fastback and saloon body styles. There were six other 800s on the stand, the saloons being represented by the 820e, 827SLi and Sterling models, with the 820i, 827SLi and Vitesse models representing the Fastback range.

The good news was that there were no price increases for the new season. There were seven new paint colours, including three metallics, of which one was actually a micatallic, which used small particles of mica within the paint to reflect light. Equipment levels were up. A glass sunroof was now standard across the range, with electric operation on the S models and above. All models now had a one-shot down function on the driver's door window, and rear headrests became standard on all the S models and the Vitesse. Leather upholstery was now an option for the Vitesse (although its leather-rimmed steering wheel now became an option), and the Vitesse now came with eight-way electric

adjustment for the driver's seat and a new high centre armrest for the driver; these latter two features also became standard on the 827SLi models.

Exhaust Catalysts

The 1989 models brought a new focus on exhaust emissions. The 2-litre engines were already compatible with unleaded fuel; now the 2.7-litre V6 came ready to use it as well. Catalytic converters had been available for some time on cars for North America, Japan, Australia and some European markets, and the Sterling now became the first British car for UK sale to have one as standard equipment.

The catalytic converter itself was a three-way closed-loop type that Rover claimed would reduce the emission of noxious gases by more than 60 per cent when compared with the non-catalyst 2.7-litre V6. By the standards of UK legislation, the engine was ultra-clean as its emissions were lower than existing legislated standards by more than 80 per cent. Cars with the catalyst were to have a narrow fuel filler neck to avoid misfuelling (pumps for unleaded fuel had a narrower nozzle than standard), and there would be reminders that the car must use only unleaded fuel on the instrument pack, the fuel cap and under the bonnet. Even the rear window would carry a discreet 'Catalyst' decal.

The cleaner catalyst engines came with certain penalties. With a lower compression ratio of 9.0:1 to prevent detonation, the catalyst V6 had only 171PS (169bhp) as against the 177PS (175bhp) of the non-catalyst engine, and Rover claimed that it took 8.9sec to power the car to 60mph from rest as against the 8.7sec of the non-catalyst version. Buyers also had to pay extra for the catalytic converter, which in practice did not become available through showrooms until December. At least the fuel consumption was said to be unchanged.

Anti-Theft Measures

Anti-theft measures were another new feature. The 1989-model Sterling now came with an anti-theft alarm as standard equipment. This alarm was optional on all other models in the range, and all models had a security coded ICE system.

Further promoting their work on anti-theft measures, Rover prepared a special Sterling saloon at the request of the Home Office to highlight their work in the area. Called

The Rover Security Concepts Car, unveiled in late 1988, introduced a number of new ideas that would later become standard, although some were not pursued.

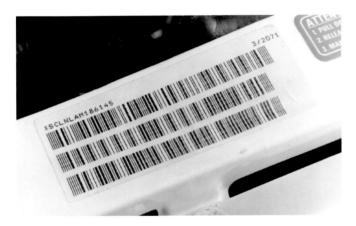

Another new idea was to present the VIN in barcode form.

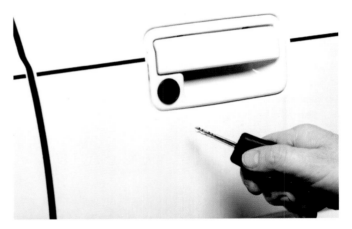

New ideas showcased included infra-red keyless door locking, a side window alarm, a continuity strip, and the registration number and VIN etched into the window glass.

the Security Concepts Car, this was presented at the Standing Conference on Crime Prevention in early December. The main emphasis of the measures it displayed was on deterring the opportunist thief, who was responsible for 70–90 per cent of all car thefts in the UK. Many of the anti-theft measures on this car would later become commonplace on new cars, including infra-red remote central locking, an externally visible VIN label, and etching of the VIN serial number and registration number onto each of the car's windows.

Cross-Range Changes, April/June 1989

Further cross-range changes arrived in April 1989, well in advance of the beginning of the 1990 model year that

autumn. The most obvious of these was to the instrument panel, where more conventional circular main dials replaced the rather fussy dials on the first cars, with just a single auxiliary gauge on either side of the panel. It made the gauges easier to read.

There was a modification to the automatic selector lever, and a new air-conditioning system with ATC (Automatic Temperature Control) – which depended on temperature sensors to meet a target temperature selected on the control panel – became available on models with the S specification and above. At the same time, ABS became an extra-cost option on all models that did not already have it.

There was one final change in June 1989, just slightly ahead of the 1990 model year. The Sterling had been available with a catalytic converter since the start of the 1989 model year; now a catalytic converter became available as an option on all other models of the range in the UK. Legislation in some export territories required catalytic converters on all new cars, so for Rover it was no great hardship to make the export specification available to environmentally conscious customers in their home market – as long as they were prepared to pay extra for it. (It may have been at this time that new '16v Catalyst' badges first appeared at the rear of 4-cylinder models thus equipped, although the catalyst specification was largely confined to export models and it is impossible to be certain at present.)

This was the new style of instrument panel for 1990, which many found much easier to read than the original.

PAINT AND TRIM OPTIONS – 1988–1989 MODELS

1988 model year

The new Fastback and Vitesse models were introduced in May 1988, right at the end of the 1988 model year.

The twelve paint options and four interior colours were the same as they had been at the start of the 1988 model year (*see* Chapter 2). However, Vitesse models were available only in four colours: Black, Pulsar Silver, Stone Grey and Targa Red, and always came with Flint interior trim and their own style of upholstery.

1989 model year

There were again twelve paint options, of which four were new: British Racing Green, Flame Red, Pearlescent Cherry Red and Steel Grey replaced Burgundy Red, Shantung Gold, Strata Grey and Targa Red.

Black and all the metallic paints cost extra except on the Vitesse and Sterling models; Pearlescent Cherry Red cost extra on all models. The Vitesse was available in only eight colours. It was not available in Azure Blue, Lynx Bronze, Oyster Beige and Steel Grey. The Sterling could be ordered with all colours, and came with Duo Tone paintwork, featuring Gunmetal lower panels; Pearlescent Cherry Red could be ordered either with or without the contrasting Gunmetal panels on the Sterling.

The four interior colours were unchanged. Entry-level upholstery (820, 820e and 820i) was in Plain Velvet; there was Chalkstripe and Plain Velvet for the 820Se, 820Si and 827Si models; the 827SLi had Diagonal and Plain Velvet, or leather at extra cost; the Vitesse had Lightning and Velvet, invariably in Flint; and the Sterling had leather as standard but could have Diagonal and Plain Velvet as a no-cost option.

PAINT AND TRIM OPTIONS FOR 1988–1989 MODELS

Paint	Interior
Atlantic Blue (metallic)	Flint or Prussian Blue
Azure Blue (metallic)	Flint or Prussian Blue
Black	Coffee Beige or Flint
British Racing Green (metallic)	Coffee Beige or Flint
Flame Red	Coffee Beige or Flint
Lynx Bronze (metallic)	Coffee Beige or Flint
Oyster Beige	Coffee Beige or Mink
Pearlescent Cherry Red	Coffee Beige or Mink
Pulsar Silver (metallic)	Flint or Mink
Steel Grey (metallic)	Flint or Mink
Stone Grey (metallic)	Coffee Beige or Flint
White Diamond	Coffee Beige or Flint

TECHNICAL SPECIFICATIONS – 1988–1989 MODELS

Engines
M8 (O-series) 4-cylinder petrol
Iron block with aluminium alloy cylinder head
1994cc (84.5 x 89mm)
Single ohc, belt-driven
2v per cylinder
Five-bearing crankshaft
Compression ratio 9.1:1
Carburettor with automatic choke
100PS (99bhp) at 5,400rpm
163Nm (120lb ft) at 3,000rpm

M16e and M16i 4-cylinder petrol
Iron block with aluminium alloy cylinder head
1994cc (84.5 x 89mm)
Twin ohc, belt-driven
4v per cylinder
Five-bearing crankshaft
Compression ratio 10.0:1
M16e
ARG throttle-body injection
120PS (118bhp) at 5,600rpm
162Nm (119lb ft) at 3,500rpm
M16i
Lucas multi-point injection
140PS (138bhp) at 6,000rpm
178Nm (131lb ft) at 4,500rpm

Honda C27A V6 petrol
Aluminium alloy block and cylinder head
2675cc (87 x 75mm)
Single ohc on each cylinder bank
4v per cylinder
Four-bearing crankshaft
Compression ratio 9.4:1
Honda PGM-FI multi-point injection
177PS (175bhp) at 6,000rpm
228Nm (168lb ft) at 4,500rpm

Transmission
Five-speed manual gearbox standard
  (4-cylinder petrol models; Honda type PG1 G6)
    Ratios 3.25:1, 1.89:1, 1.22:1, 0.93:1, 0.76:1; reverse 3.00:1

(V6 models; Honda type PG2)
Ratios 2.92:1, 1.79:1, 1.22:1, 0.91:1, 0.75:1; reverse 3.00:1

Four-speed automatic gearbox optional
  (4-cylinder models; ZF type 4HP 14)
  Ratios 2.41:1, 1.37:1, 1.00:1, 0.74:1; reverse 2.83:1
  (V6 models; Honda type EAT)
  Ratios 2.65:1, 1.55:1, 0.06:1, 0.79:1; reverse 1.90:1

Axle ratio
4.20:1   4-cylinder petrol and V6 models with manual
        gearbox
4.27:1   V6 automatic models
4.40:1   4-cylinder petrol models with automatic gearbox

Suspension, steering and brakes
Front suspension with unequal length double wishbones,
  steel coil springs and elastomeric compound spring aids,
  co-axial telescopic dampers and anti-roll bar
Rear suspension with independent struts, transverse
  and trailing links, steel coil springs and elastomeric
  compound spring aids, telescopic dampers and
  anti-roll bar. Boge Nivomat self-levelling dampers
  standard on 827SLi saloon and Sterling; optional
  on both Fastback and saloon models of 820e, 820i,
  820Se, 820Si and 827Si; not available on 820 Fastback
  or Vitesse
Rack-and-pinion steering with power assistance as standard:
  TRW Cam Gears type PCF on 4-cylinder models; Honda
  speed proportional type on V6 models
Disc brakes all round, with single-cylinder floating calipers;
  handbrake acting on rear discs
Ventilated front discs with 262mm diameter on 4-cylinder
  models and 285mm diameter on V6 models
Solid rear discs with 260mm diameter on all models
Two diagonally split hydraulic circuits; ABS standard on
  Vitesse and optional on all other models except 820

Dimensions
Overall length   184.8in (4,694mm)
Overall width   68.1in (1,730mm)
                    76.6in (1,946mm) over mirrors
Overall height   55in (1,398mm)

TECHNICAL SPECIFICATIONS – 1988–1989 MODELS (continued)

Wheelbase 108.6in (2,759mm)
Front track 58.7in (1,492mm)
Rear track 57.1in (1,450mm)

Wheels and tyres

5.5J x 14 steel wheels with 175 HR 14 tyres on 820

6J x 14 steel wheels with 195/70 HR 14 tyres on 'e' and 'i' models

6J x 15 steel wheels with 195/65 VR 15 tyres on S models

6J x 15 alloy wheels with 195/65 VR 15 tyres on V6 models except Vitesse

6J x 15 alloy wheels with 205/60 VR 15 tyres on Vitesse model

Kerb weight

2,866lb (1,300kg)	820 Fastback
2,944lb (1,335kg)	820e Fastback
2,988lb (1,355kg)	820Se Fastback
2,933lb (1,330kg)	820i Fastback
2,977lb (1,350kg)	820Si Fastback
3,098lb (1,405kg)	827Si Fastback
3,142lb (1,425kg)	Vitesse Fastback

Add 34lb (15kg) in each case for automatic gearbox.

PERFORMANCE AND FUEL CONSUMPTION FIGURES – 1988–1989 MODELS

These figures are the ones claimed by the manufacturer.

	0–60mph	Maximum speed	Fuel consumption
820 Fastback manual	11.6sec	112mph (180km/h)	34.8mpg (8.1ltr/100km)
820 Fastback automatic	13.5sec	110mph (177km/h)	33.3mpg (8.5ltr/100km)
820e and Se manual	10.5sec	120mph (193km/h) Fastback 119mph (191km/h) Saloon	35.3mpg (8ltr/100km)
820e and Se automatic	11.9sec	118mph (190km/h) Fastback 117mph (188km/h) Saloon	31.9mpg (8.9ltr/100km)
820i and Si manual	9.2sec	127mph (204km/h) Fastback 126mph (202km/h) Saloon	33.9mpg (8.3ltr/100km)
827Si manual	7.6sec	138mph (222km/h) Fastback 137mph (220km/h) Saloon	29.6mpg (9.6ltr/100km)
827Si automatic	8.7sec	134mph (215km/h)	27.5mpg (10.3ltr/100km)
Sterling automatic	8.7sec	134mph (215km/h)	27.5mpg (10.3ltr/100km)
Vitesse manual	7.6sec	140mph (225km/h)	29.6mpg (9.6ltr/100km)
Vitesse automatic	8.5sec	135mph (217km/h)	27.5mpg (10.3ltr/100km)

CHAPTER FOUR

DIESELS AND TURBOS

The first three years of Rover 800 production had seen Rover expand the range by the introduction of a second body variant in the shape of the Fastback. This in turn had allowed the introduction of a sporty derivative (the Vitesse) and a lower-priced entry model (the 820). Despite a series of setbacks, work was going ahead on a third model as well, this time a coupé that would eventually see the light of day in 1992 (see Chapter 8).

The initial engine line-up of 2-litre M16e and M16i engines, plus the 2.5-litre Honda V6, had also been expanded. The 2-litre O-series engine had been introduced for the entry-level 820 models, while the original 2.5-litre Honda engine had been replaced by a 2.7-litre version. Yet there were still gaps in the 800 range that needed to be filled and, as the 1990s opened, Rover set about filling them.

The major gaps were in two areas. First, the 800 range had no diesel model, even though the SD1 range it replaced had done well in countries such as France, Italy and the Netherlands in diesel-engined form after 1982. The wait for a diesel model must have been enormously frustrating for Rover dealers in those countries, especially in France, where almost half the large cars sold were powered by diesel engines – by the turn of the decade, France was Rover's biggest export market. Second, the 800 range lacked a convincing performance model. The Vitesse, introduced in 1988, had no better acceleration than other V6-engined 800s because its 2.7-litre V6 engine was in exactly the same state of tune. The buyers were not impressed, and Rover knew that it had to make amends as quickly as possible.

On the diesel front, Rover knew what they wanted to do quite early on but the project was delayed by the search for a suitable gearbox. 'Finding, adapting and proving the right 'box … accounted for much of the new model's lengthy gestation period,' reported *Diesel Car* magazine in September 1990, when the new 825D model finally arrived. On the high-performance front, there were simply no resources available to improve the Vitesse or to engineer an alter-

native. In the late 1980s, Rover product development staff were heavily focused on the forthcoming R8 small saloons, which emerged as the 200 series in 1989 and the 400 series in 1990. These cars brought with them a brand-new engine, the K-series. Delivering them on time meant that there were limited resources available for the improvement of the 800 range, so the larger cars just had to wait their turn.

So it was that no diesel model appeared until summer 1990, and no new high-performance derivative appeared until nine months after that. By that stage, the 800 range had nearly reached the midpoint of its planned production run and a major facelift was just a few months away. As a result, the new high-performance model that did appear in March 1991 could only be a low-volume 'teaser' anticipating what might come later. It was squeezed into the engineering programme only by subcontracting its development to an outside company.

THE 1990 MODELS

During the summer of 1989 new Rover Group branding began to appear on company literature. Until that point, there had been Austin Rover branding on press releases and sales brochures had carried the Rover Viking ship badge. For 1990, a bold maroon rectangle with the Rover name in capitals became the new norm. This new branding arrived to coincide with the introduction of the new R8 200 models, which kept Rover busy at the start of the 1990 model year.

Nevertheless, this was far from a fallow time for the 800 range. Larger bumpers became standard, making the cars some 4in longer, and a new range of wheel trim styles and alloy wheels was introduced, with designs largely intended to match their counterparts on the new R8 200 series cars. A body-colour rear spoiler became standard on all Fastbacks, including the 820. The 4-cylinder cars now had '16v' badges at the rear to advertise the benefits of their 16-valve

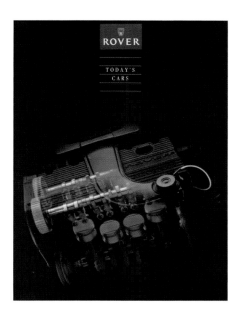

The new Rover logo introduced for the 1990 model year is seen here on a 1990 sales catalogue. Rover was promoting a high-tech image with the 'ghosted' picture of its twin-cam M16 engine.

Green tinted glass became standard, with a windscreen shade band on S models and above. The base model 820 gained a driver's footrest, and S-specification models gained map pockets on the front seat backs, with burr walnut inserts in the centre console. The number of interior colour options was reduced by one, as Coffee Beige was dropped. The Vitesse now became available in a wider range of colours, and there was some shuffling of the pricing on various paint options. So Black and the metallic paints came at extra cost, and the new Pearlescent Cherry Red (a micatallic) cost even more – unless it was ordered for a Vitesse or a Sterling, when the price was discounted.

Meanwhile, some changes to gearbox availability were probably intended to help streamline production. In the

engines, which at the time were still quite new in terms of technology. When fitted with a catalytic converter, as available for the M16i and V6 engines, the badge read '16v Catalyst'. The V6 models took on '24v' badges, although these were not accompanied by a catalyst indicator. Self-levelling disappeared from the specification of the 827SLi, but remained available as an option.

This was the 1990 line-up of ICE options for the UK market. From top to bottom, they are: R984 CD/tuner, R682 stereo radio-cassette with RDS, R681 stereo radio-cassette and R670 stereo radio-cassette. All were of Philips manufacture.

For 1990, the number of valves in the engine became an important marketing tool. V6 models took on '24v' badges like the one seen on this Vitesse.

UK, the automatic option was reintroduced for the 820i and 820Si models after an absence of nearly three years, this time with a catalytic converter as standard equipment. In the UK, however, the automatic 820i and automatic 820 were now available only to order, as were manual-gearbox versions of the 827Si, 827SLi and Sterling models.

There were plenty of options to tempt 800 customers for 1990. Both saloon and Fastback variants could be had with the body styling kit, which for additional cost could be painted to suit the two-tone finish of the Sterling. There were 16in alloy wheels to go with it. Fastback models, but not saloons, could have a sports suspension pack, which was simply the suspension developed for the Vitesse; self-levelling rear suspension was another option. On the inside the cars could be fitted with rear head restraints, an uprated R681 ICE head unit and a power amplifier to make the most of that.

Automatic gearboxes, ABS brakes, an anti-theft alarm and a catalytic converter all cost extra, too. So did air conditioning with ATC, alloy wheels with 195/65 VR tyres, and a headlamp power-wash system. Leather upholstery normally came with power adjustment for the driver's seat, but on saloons only it was possible to have it without that refinement.

Saloon and Fastback ranges were carefully priced so that directly equivalent versions cost the same, while the 820 Fastback remained an entry-level model and the Vitesse and Sterling were very different top models with different prices. As at 26 September 1989, the UK price range for models without extras was as follows:

	Saloon	Fastback
820		£13,785
820e	£14,375	£14,375
820i	£15,740	£15,740
820Se	£15,850	£15,850
820Si	£17,215	£17,215
827Si	£18,600	£18,600
827SLi	£20,675	
Vitesse		£22,390
Sterling	£24,870	

Getting the message out there: Rover provided examples of the latest 800 range as courtesy cars for the 1990 British Open Golf Championship. Each one carried the latest Rover logo prominently on its bonnet.

**Rover provided a fleet of courtesy 800s
for the Wimbledon tennis championships
over the summer of 1990, too.**

**More publicity activity: two Rover 800s
carried the teams in the EEC challenge.**

A VITESSE ON THE TT CIRCUIT

The original Rover Vitesse had been created as a homologation special so that the car could go racing, and its success on the race tracks between 1982 and 1986 gave the car an image that guaranteed strong sales – even though buyers knew that Rover build quality was often substandard. As the Vitesse version of the 800 range was not going to have a motor sport programme to reinforce its credibility, the Rover Group settled on another way to boost its performance credentials.

The plan was for former rally driver Tony Pond to attempt the first-ever 100mph lap of the Isle of Man TT motorcycle circuit in a standard production car. At that stage, Pond was working as a development driver for the Rover Group. The attempt was made in June 1988, just a month after the new Vitesse had been announced, but it failed. *Motor* magazine had been there to witness the occasion and had reserved space for a report in its issue of 25 June. Unfortunately, heavy rain slowed progress in the mountain section of the circuit and Pond missed the planned 100mph lap by just 6.8sec. The *Motor* report was as positive as it could be in the circumstances, but the Vitesse did not get the major publicity boost that had been planned.

By 1990, Vitesse sales were flagging and the model was desperately in need of an image boost. So the idea of that 100mph TT lap attempt was revived. On 6 June 1990 Pond and a Vitesse were ready to go. The car, not surprisingly finished in eye-catching red, was standard in all respects except for its racing tyres, special brake pads and internal safety cage.

Wet weather very nearly also put paid to this second attempt. The original plan had been to fit it in just before the Senior TT race, but on the day it had to be delayed until 6pm. This time, however, Pond and the Vitesse were successful, achieving an average speed of 102.19mph (164.47km/h) over the 37.73-mile (60.72-km) course and lapping in 22min 9.1sec. The car clocked 150mph (241km/h) through Highlander, the fastest part of the TT circuit, and the record stood until 2011. The record run was recorded by cameras mounted on the car, and a promotional film was later released.

Did it achieve its publicity objectives? Possibly, but less than two years later a much more convincingly sporty 800 derivative was needed to persuade the buying public that the big Rover could be a performance car as well as a comfortable saloon.

THE TRANSWORLD VENTURE

Rover provided the cars for another record attempt in June 1990, so keeping the 800 in the headlines. The Transworld Venture was co-sponsored by Michelin and others, and involved two Army teams of three drivers beating the existing record of sixty-nine days to drive around the world.

The cars were a pair of left-hand-drive 827Si saloons (registered as G996 XHP and G997 XHP), shod with the latest Michelin XM+S 300 tyres. They were mechanically standard, but were prepared at BL's Gaydon premises with additional lighting, underfloor shielding, reinforced fuel tanks, radiator stone-guards and roo bars so that they could survive some of the rough roads that would form part of the journey. The interiors were configured so that the third crew member could sleep while the other two drove and navigated.

The two Transworld Rover 800s are seen here with their crews and support team.

The two cars left from the Tower of London on 13 May and completed their circumnavigation of the globe on 22 June. They had taken 39 days, 23 hours and 35 minutes to travel a distance of 26,078 miles (41,968km), which publicity for the event claimed had been entirely free of any mechanical troubles. One of the cars was later handed over to the museum collection at the Heritage Motor Centre (now British Motor Museum) in Gaydon.

FACING UP TO THE OPPOSITION

During 1989, UK sales of the Rover 800 overtook those of the Ford Granada, which had previously led the class. Ford fought back quickly by introducing in 1990 a three-box saloon alternative to the original Granada hatchback. *Autocar & Motor* magazine (the two were now combined into one) compared the top model Ghia X of this range, with its 150bhp 2.9-litre V6 engine, against a 1990-model 827Si saloon.

From the start, the prices showed the Rover to have an advantage – it cost £19,455 with extras, against £20,895 for

the Ford – and the magazine found the Rover to have an almost crushing superiority.

'The Granada looks frumpy and drives like it,' they said. 'Alongside the Rover it's too soft, under-damped, under-powered and unrefined. ... If there's a saving grace it's the ride, which betters the Rover's at most speeds provided it isn't pushed too hard.' On performance, 'the Rover easily outpaces the Ford', and the handling advantage also lay with the 827: 'the Granada is a big car that feels it; the 827 somehow conceals its bulk and feels like a GTi by comparison.'

Lastly, the Rover also came out ahead on its appearance, with some slight reservations. 'Its decisive, razor-edge styling makes the Ford appear a clumsy effort … [but] the Granada can look impressive from some angles … while the Rover is just a touch anonymous.' So even though sales of the Rover were beginning to slide, it still stacked up very well against its main opposition, a car that had been released onto the market just a year before it in 1985.

DEVELOPING THE DIESEL 800

It had been clear from the early days of the XX project that Rover would need a diesel-powered derivative of the 800 range if it was to maintain sales of the range on the European continent. Although diesel cars were still treated with a great deal of caution by British buyers, the lower running costs of diesel engines had endeared them to buyers across the Channel since the middle of the 1970s and a diesel engine was an important option in any range of large (and therefore potentially thirsty) cars.

The Italian diesel engine maker VM Motori, based at Cento near Bologna, recognized that the move towards diesel engines had caught many car makers without such an engine. They therefore developed a new range of engines to fill the gap, known as the HR-series. These were designed to suit industrial and marine applications as well as passenger cars and, following VM's time-honoured principles, they had a modular design that allowed maximum flexibility of variants. So, using a common bore and stroke, the company could build 4-cylinder, 5-cylinder and 6-cylinder versions of the same engine. One result of this modular design was that the HR-series engines always had a separate head for each cylinder. All of them were designed to be turbocharged for automotive applications.

The industrial and marine versions of the HR range were announced in 1978, and the automotive version was shown for the first time a year later at the Frankfurt Motor Show. It was exactly the right engine at exactly the right time: during 1979 the second Oil Crisis pushed fuel prices up alarmingly and the general public began to look upon diesel car engines in a new light.

By this stage, VM had already made approaches to a number of car manufacturers. Among those they approached was British Leyland, which at that stage was high and dry without a diesel car engine or even the plans for one. A diesel strategy for the company's bigger (and therefore thirstier) cars soon fell into place. The 2.4-litre 4-cylinder HR engine would go into the Rover SD1 saloon; the 3-litre 5-cylinder version would go into the Range Rover; and the 3.6-litre 6-cylinder would go into the Jaguar XJ6. From BL's point of view, this made perfect sense, given that the engines shared many common components so the supply of spare parts would be simplified.

In the UK, the new diesel model was available only in low-specification form as an 825D, but there were better-equipped models for overseas markets, which were more attuned to diesel engines in large cars.

The four separate cylinder heads of the VM diesel engine were concealed under a cover that carried both VM and Rover branding.

The plan did not quite work out that way in practice. The Range Rover eventually took an intercooled version of the 4-cylinder engine and Jaguar shied away from diesel altogether. Nevertheless, the link between VM and BL had been established, and the Italian company was able to exploit it. In a further development of the HR-series, they increased the stroke so that the 4-cylinder engine became a 2.5-litre, and from 1989 the Land Rover division of British Leyland put that into Range Rovers.

The new 2.5-litre VM engine was a more or less natural choice for the diesel 800 Series, although its installation was less straightforward than in the Range Rover for two reasons. Most obviously, the engine had to be adapted to suit the transverse installation demanded by the 800 Series layout. Then a problem arose because the existing 800 Series manual gearboxes could not handle the high torque of the diesel engine. This introduced a delay into the programme while a suitable alternative was sought. Rover eventually settled on the five-speed A568 type made by New Venture Gears in the USA, a company owned by the Chrysler Corporation; this was also known in Rover literature as the T650 gearbox.

The basic version of the engine was the same as that already available in the Alfa Romeo 164, and was known as an HR494 type. As installed in the Rover, it delivered 118PS (116bhp) at 4,200rpm and 268Nm (198lb ft) of torque at 2,100rpm. It also had a plastic cylinder head cover bearing the Rover name that concealed its distinctive individual cylinder heads, which made a great improvement over the rather untidy under-bonnet view of the diesel-engined Rover SD1.

THE 1991 MODELS

The diesel 800 was released on 19 June 1990. There were three models, an 825D Turbo Fastback, with equipment levels comparable to the 820e and 820i models, and an 825SD Turbo that came as either Fastback or saloon with the S level of equipment. The first cars were destined for Belgium, France, the Netherlands and Spain, where Rover judged the greatest need to be. Sales would begin in Britain, and in the engine's native Italy, in September. The British market received only the 825D Turbo model at this stage, as buyers were still resistant to diesel engines in executive cars.

Although the diesels were the big news at the Birmingham NEC Motor Show that autumn, there were several other changes to the 800 range. A new 820SLi model arrived with the enhanced S specification of the 827SLi, and the entry-level petrol models were all quietly dropped. Out went the 820 Fastback with its unique O-series engine, and out went the 820e and 820Se with their throttle-body injection engines. The range was now a little easier to understand:

PRICES – 1991 MODELS

Prices of Rover 800 models for the 1991 model year, inclusive of taxes, were as follows at 18 September 1990:

820i	Saloon/Fastback	£16,325
825D Turbo	Fastback	£17,930
820Si	Saloon/Fastback	£18,085
820SLi	Saloon/Fastback	£18,890
827Si	Saloon/Fastback	£20,270
827SLi	Saloon/Fastback	£23,730
Sterling	Saloon	£25,995
Vitesse	Fastback	£25,995

This was the 1991-model 820i Fastback, with wheel trims new for the new season. Rover publicity was putting special emphasis on the Fastbacks in the UK at the time and all the press pictures showed them rather than saloons.

there were entry-level models (820i and 825D); S-specification models (820Si and 825SD); SL-specification models (820SLi and 827SLi); the Sterling to top the saloon range; and the Vitesse to top the Fastback range.

A new and wider range of paint options became available, accompanied by a (mostly) new range of upholstery colours. There were new styles of upholstery fabric on the entry-level, S and SLi models, too. Right across the range, a delay system on the headlamps and courtesy lights meant that they remained on for a few seconds after the ignition had been turned off. Entry-level models came with a Philips R670 radio-cassette ICE head unit, the S models had an R681 type, the SLi had an R682 and the Vitesse and Sterling came with an R684 radio-CD player.

At the bottom of the range, the 820i gained an anti-theft alarm and programmed wash-wipe as standard. The S models took on a one-shot passenger door window and a larger clock for 1991, while UK buyers were offered an 827SLi in Fastback form for the first time. The saloon and Fastback versions of the 827SLi now came with ABS and ATC air conditioning as standard, while the saloon models came with Duo Tone paintwork. The Vitesse was given added appeal with leather upholstery as standard, plus electrically adjusted and heated front seats and a memory for the driver's seat and door mirror positions. The Sterling, meanwhile, now came with revised piping and stitching for its leather upholstery and ignition-off electric seat adjustment.

This 1991-model Vitesse has the optional 16in Roversport alloy wheels – the only wheels on the 800 series not to carry Rover badges.

The SLi models had coachlines on the flanks and bright finishes on the bump-strips. This style of alloy wheel was new for the 1991 model year.

The saloon models remained available, of course, and this is a 1991 820i model.

OPTIONAL EXTRAS – 1991 MODELS

The following extra-cost options for the UK market were listed on 18 September 1990. Some items were standard on the more expensive derivatives.

ABS
Alloy wheels (15in)
Alloy wheels: 16in Roversport five-spoke design
Alloy wheels: 16in type recommended with body styling kit
ATC air conditioning
Automatic gearbox
Body styling kit
Catalytic converter

Connolly leather seat trim
Electric pack
Headlamp power wash
ICE: R681 instead of R670
ICE: R682 instead of R670
ICE: R682 instead of R681
ICE: R984 (radio/CD) instead of R670
ICE: R984 instead of R681
Paint: Black, metallic or pearlescent
Rear head restraints
Self-levelling rear suspension
Sports pack (Fastback only)

THE 825D AND THE PRESS

When the diesel version of the 800 was introduced, British enthusiasm for diesel cars still lagged a long way behind that on the European continent. *Diesel Car* magazine was a pioneering UK publication that focused on what its title suggested. It always seemed to express a real delight when it tested a genuinely good new diesel model, and the Rover 825D it tested in its September 1990 issue was such a car. It was, they wrote, 'an outstanding car that will surely have some big names in diesel distinctly worried'. Fuel consumption was on the right side of 35mpg (8ltr/100km) and the engine did not smoke (which was far from the case with many rival diesels), although it did require a rather long warm-up period for the glow plugs when cold.

> *At last we have a genuine 120mph diesel. Rover only claims 118mph, but in zero-wind conditions the test car averaged 120.3mph around the banked Millbrook bowl.*

Although the 825D could not match Rover's 0–60mph claim of 10.5sec and actually took 11.5sec, 'that's quicker than any other diesel we've tested, bar the now defunct [Citroën] CX'. *Diesel Car* reported that the Rover 'really does feel a seriously quick car, with a lot more driver appeal than the average two litre petrol executive'.

ABOVE: **The 820SLi was a new model for 1991. The 4-cylinder cars had carried '16v Catalyst' badges on the right-hand rear reflector since the 1990 model year.**

Careful lighting has been used to enhance this view of a 1991 Sterling interior, but there is no doubting the luxurious ambience created by the model's leather upholstery.

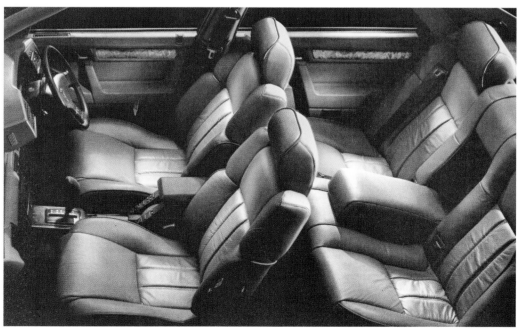

The VM engine's massive torque allows swift, effortless acceleration without any need to change down, unless you're in a real hurry. … Hard acceleration … produces a fair amount of mechanical thrash, but it's by no means loud: driven more normally the car is smooth and quiet enough for unsuspecting passengers not to realize it's a diesel. The long gearing helps make fast motorway cruising especially impressive; at 80mph the engine is turning at just 2,800rpm, and is hardly audible.

The new gearbox was 'easy and pleasant to use. There's a trace of notchiness, but movements are light and the gate is well defined.' And, in common with other 800s of the time, the car had been well built: 'This 825 had the glossiest paint finish of any test car we can remember and seemed well put together.'

THE 820 TURBO 16V – THE 'TICKFORD TURBO'

Production figures show that demand for the 800 Series had peaked in 1988 and had been dropping ever since – during 1990 they were barely half the 1988 figure. A decline such as this, so early in the 800's life, indicated that something quite radical would have to be done. In a few years, it would

become clear that sales of large cars generally were declining, but for the moment Rover had to assume that it would be possible to bring 800 sales back up to their former levels with the right changes to the product.

A major facelift and engineering revisions were already under way and were intended for introduction in autumn 1991 as the 1992 models. In the meantime, the Rover Group marketing department called for something to inject some life into 800 sales ahead of the facelifted car's arrival. What they got was the legendary 'Tickford Turbo' – more formally an 820 Turbo 16v – which former marketing man Ian Elliott confirms was intended as a 'temporary, low-budget image-booster' for the 800 range. Whether it made much difference to sales is doubtful: a lot of the cars ended up being allocated to Rover Group managers because sales were slow. Canny private buyers seem to have preferred to wait until the rumoured new models arrived in the autumn before splashing out on a new 800.

By the start of the 1990s, Rover was already planning to replace the Honda V6 engine in the Vitesse with a more powerful turbocharged 2-litre 4-cylinder that was being developed from the existing M16 type. Development was on schedule to put this new turbocharged engine into the facelifted 1992 range that would be introduced in autumn 1991, but the timing was quite tight. So when the marketing team asked if the turbocharged engine and its uprated gearbox with torsen differential could be made available

The 820 Turbo was a stop-gap model to improve the image of the 800 series at the end of the 1991 model year, just before the facelifted models became available. It could be had in both saloon and Fastback forms, with the Roversport wheels as standard.

earlier in order to give them the high-performance model the 800 range needed, the answer was a firm 'No'.

Nor was help available from Rover Special Products, which had been established as a dedicated engineering team responsible for low-volume products. So marketing and engineering teams reached a compromise, which was to develop a turbocharged version of the existing M16 engine. It would not, and could not, have all the features planned for the later turbocharged car, but it could incorporate enough of them to act as a convincing trailblazer.

Mainstream Product Engineering developed the concept, but had neither the time nor the resources to take it any further. So the detail development was subcontracted to Tickford at Bedworth, who also built some of the low-volume components special to the car. Tickford, owned by Aston Martin, had started life as the coachbuilder Salmons & Sons, but the name had been revived in 1981 as a specialist vehicle division of the main company.

The deal was similar to the one that Rover had done with Tickford for the 1989-model MG Maestro Turbo, although for the 800 the final assembly would all be done at Cowley. To get the ignition timing they needed, Tickford engineers replaced the M16's standard engine management system with a Lucas hot-wire mass-flow injection system with two separate ECUs. The fuel ECU was a 4-cylinder version of the 14CUX type then in use on the Range Rover's V8 engine, and the main ECU was

This was the engine bay of the 820 Turbo. Essentially, it looked like that of an 820Si, but nestling down in front of the engine was the turbocharger …

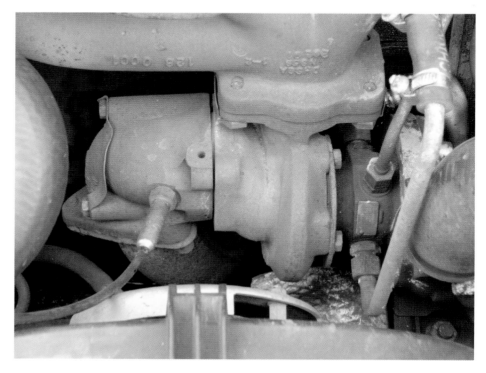

… which looked like this in close-up.

THE 820I AND 820SI SPECIAL EDITIONS, 1991

In the UK, special editions based on the 820i and 820Si saloons were introduced in May 1991. These were probably intended to help dealers move showroom stocks of the old models before the new ones became available in the autumn. These cars had a Zender body styling kit with a unique rear spoiler. They had grey ruched leather seats and door trims, an 820 Turbo steering wheel and rear head restraints as standard. There was no model badge on the boot lid. It is not clear how many of these were built.

THOUGHTS ABOUT A ROVER 800 REPLACEMENT

Work on the eventual successor to a new car very often begins as that new car enters production, and Honda were quick off the mark with starting on an eventual replacement for the Legend twin of the 800. As they were fully entitled to do, they undertook this work without any input from the Rover Group, who were far too busy working on the Fastback and (longer-term) coupé to develop any plans for an eventual 800 replacement.

Information about the planned second-generation Legend was passed to Rover during 1989. It included the revelation that Honda intended to use an engine mounted north-south rather than transversely as in the first-generation car. The Japanese company was quite happy to field Rover's interest in this new platform, and for a while during 1989 there were discussions about a Rover version that might use the Honda V6 for top models and Rover's own 2-litre engines for the larger-volume models.

It soon became apparent that a Rover version of the new Honda Legend was not a realistic option. Honda had drawn up the car so that the drive to its front wheels passed through the engine crankcase. Modifying the existing Rover engines to suit this layout was simply not going to be feasible, so Honda pressed on with their new Legend independently of Rover.

Nevertheless, a future Rover 800 replacement remained among the products in the memorandum of understanding that Honda and Rover had signed. As time moved on, it became clear that Honda were no longer interested in completely joint projects, such as the 800 had been, but that they would be more than happy to collaborate with Rover on a paid basis, in effect providing its R&D teams as support for the Rover design and engineering staff.

During 1991, there were changes in the Rover top management. Sir Graham Day (who had been knighted in 1989) moved from Rover to become chairman of parent company British Aerospace when Professor Rowland Smith retired. In his place came George Simpson. Simpson had been Rover's managing director since January 1989, having earlier been with Leyland-DAF, and he quickly appointed John Towers, formerly the sales director, as his successor.

There had been changes in the top management at Honda, too, and before long the five products in the memorandum of understanding were given new names. These all had an SK prefix, which apparently stood for the names Simpson and Kawamoto. SK5 was to be the new big Rover – but there were more pressing projects within the Rover Group and the plan never turned into a formal project, eventually disappearing from the forward products schedule after BMW bought Rover in 1994.

PAINT AND TRIM OPTIONS – 1990–1991 MODELS

1990 model year

The twelve paint options were unchanged from the 1989 season. Black and all the metallic paints cost extra except on the Vitesse and Sterling models; Pearlescent Cherry Red cost extra on all models. The Vitesse was available only in eight colours: Azure Blue, Lynx Bronze, Oyster Beige and Steel Grey were not available on these cars. The Sterling could be ordered with all colours, and came with Duo Tone paintwork, featuring Gunmetal lower panels except when Black or Steel Grey was specified.

There were now just three interior colours, Coffee Beige having been dropped. Entry-level upholstery (820, 820e and 820i) was in Zenith and Plain Velvet; there was Chalkstripe and Plain Velvet for the 820Se, 820Si and 827Si models; the 827SLi had Diagonal and Plain Velvet, or leather at extra cost; the Vitesse had Lightning and leather or plain leather, invariably in Flint; and the Sterling had leather as standard but could have Diagonal and Plain Velvet as a no-cost option.

PAINT AND TRIM OPTIONS FOR 1990 MODELS

Paint	Interior
Atlantic Blue	Flint or Prussian Blue
Azure Blue	Flint or Prussian Blue
Black	Flint
British Racing Green	Flint
Flame Red	Flint
Lynx Bronze	Flint
Oyster Beige	Mink
Pearlescent Cherry Red	Mink
Pulsar Silver	Flint or Mink
Steel Grey	Flint or Mink
Stone Grey	Flint
White Diamond	Flint

1991 model year

There were thirteen paint colours available. Black and metallic paints were a no-cost option for the Vitesse and Sterling, but cost extra on all other 800 models. Pearlescent Caribbean Blue and Pearlescent Nightfire were available only at extra cost. The 827SLi (but not 820SLi) and Sterling came with Gunmetal lower contrast panels but could be ordered without them when painted in one of the two pearlescent colours.

There were now six interior colours. Cloth was available in Granite, Prussian Blue and Stone Beige; leather came in Light Granite, Light Stone Beige or Prussian Blue; Black was available only on the 820 Turbo.

Entry-level upholstery was in Renaissance fabric; the S specification brought Chevron fabric; and leather was standard on the Vitesse and Sterling. The two top models could have Chevron upholstery at no extra cost, while leather was an extra-cost option for the S-specification cars. Leather was also used for saloon versions of the 820 Turbo 16v and the Fastback versions of that model had special half-leather upholstery as used earlier on the Vitesse.

PAINT AND TRIM OPTIONS FOR 1991 MODELS

Paint	Availability	Interior
Amethyst (metallic)	Not Vitesse	Prussian Blue
Atlantic Blue (metallic)	Not Vitesse	Prussian Blue
Black	All models	Stone Beige or Light Stone Beige
British Racing Green (metallic)	All models	Stone Beige or Light Stone Beige
Cranberry Red	Not Vitesse	Stone Beige or Light Stone Beige
Flame Red	All models	Granite or Light Granite
Midnight Blue	Not Vitesse	Prussian Blue
Nordic Bue (metallic)	Not Vitesse	Granite or Light Granite
Pearlescent Caribbean Blue	All models	Granite or Light Granite
Pearlescent Nightfire	All models	Granite or Light Granite
Quicksilver (metallic)	All models	Granite or Light Granite
Storm Grey (metallic)	All models	Granite or Light Granite
White Diamond	All models	Granite or Light Granite

TECHNICAL SPECIFICATIONS – 1990–1991 MODELS

Engines
M8 (O-series) 4-cylinder petrol (1990 models only)
Iron block with aluminium alloy cylinder head
1994cc (84.5 x 89mm)
Single ohc, belt-driven
2v per cylinder
Five-bearing crankshaft
Compression ratio 9.1:1
Carburettor with automatic choke
100PS (99bhp) at 5,400rpm
163Nm (120lb ft) at 3,000rpm

M16e and M16i 4-cylinder petrol
Iron block with aluminium alloy cylinder head
1994cc (84.5 x 89mm)
Twin ohc, belt-driven
4v per cylinder
Five-bearing crankshaft
Compression ratio 10.0:1
M16e
ARG throttle-body injection
120PS (118bhp) at 5,600rpm
162Nm (119lb ft) at 3,500rpm
M16i
Lucas multi-point injection
140PS (138bhp) at 6,000rpm (135PS with catalytic converter)
178Nm (131lb ft) at 4,500rpm

M16 turbocharged 4-cylinder petrol (1991 820 Turbo
16v only)
Iron block with aluminium alloy cylinder head
1994cc (84.5 x 89mm)
Twin ohc, belt-driven
4v per cylinder
Five-bearing crankshaft
Compression ratio N/k
Lucas multi-point injection
180PS (178bhp) at 6,000rpm
Torque N/k

Honda C27A V6 petrol
Aluminium alloy block and cylinder head
2675cc (87 x 75mm)
Single ohc on each cylinder bank
4v per cylinder
Four-bearing crankshaft
Compression ratio 9.4:1

Honda PGM-FI multi-point injection
177PS (175bhp) at 6,000rpm (171PS with catalytic converter)
228Nm (168lb ft) at 4,500rpm

VM HR 494 4-cylinder diesel (type 4924 SHI RG) (1991
models only)
Iron block with four individual aluminium alloy cylinder heads
2498cc (92 x 94mm)
Overhead valves
Five-bearing crankshaft
Compression ratio 22.1:1
KKK turbocharger with intercooler and indirect injection
118PS (116bhp) at 4,200rpm
268Nm (198lb ft) at 2,100rpm

Transmission
Five-speed manual gearbox standard
    (4-cylinder petrol models; type PG1 G6)
    Ratios 3.25:1, 1.89:1, 1.22:1, 0.93:1, 0.76:1; reverse 3.00:1
    (Diesel models; New Venture Gears type A568/T650)
    Ratios 3.00:1, 1.89:1, 1.28:1, 0.94:1, 0.72:1; reverse 3.14:1
    (V6 models; Honda type PG2)
    Ratios 2.92:1, 1.79:1, 1.22:1, 0.91:1, 0.75:1; reverse 3.00:1

Four-speed automatic gearbox optional
    (4-cylinder models; ZF type 4HP 14)
    Ratios 2.41:1, 1.37:1, 1.00:1, 0.74:1; reverse 2.83:1
    (V6 models; Honda type EAT)
    Ratios 2.65:1, 1.55:1, 0.06:1, 0.79:1; reverse 1.90:1

Axle ratio
3.50:1   Diesel models
4.20:1   4-cylinder petrol and V6 models with manual
          gearbox
4.27:1   V6 automatic models
4.40:1   4-cylinder petrol models with automatic gearbox

Suspension, steering and brakes
Front suspension with unequal length double wishbones,
    steel coil springs and elastomeric compound spring aids,
    co-axial telescopic dampers and anti-roll bar
Rear suspension with independent struts, transverse and
    trailing links, steel coil springs and elastomeric compound
    spring aids, telescopic dampers and anti-roll bar. Boge
    Nivomat self-levelling dampers standard on Sterling;
    optional on both Fastback and saloon models of 820e,
    820i, 820Se, 820Si, 827Si and 827SLi; not available on 820
    Fastback or Vitesse

TECHNICAL SPECIFICATIONS – 1990–1991 MODELS *(continued)*

Rack-and-pinion steering with power assistance as standard: TRW Cam Gears type PCF on 4-cylinder models; Honda speed proportional type on V6 models

Disc brakes all round, with single-cylinder floating calipers; handbrake acting on rear discs

Ventilated front discs with 262mm diameter on 4-cylinder models and 285mm diameter on V6 and 820 Turbo 16v models.

Solid rear discs with 260mm diameter on all models

Two diagonally split hydraulic circuits; ABS standard on Vitesse and optional on all other models except 820.

Dimensions

Overall length	189in (4,800mm)
Overall width	68.1in (1,730mm)
	76.6in (1,946mm) over mirrors
Overall height	55in (1,398mm)
Wheelbase	108.6in (2,759mm)
Front track	58.7in (1,492mm)
Rear track	57.1in (1,450mm)

Wheels and tyres:

5.5J x 14 steel wheels with 175 HR 14 tyres on 820

6J x 14 steel wheels with 195/70 HR 14 tyres on 'e' and 'i' models

6J x 15 steel wheels with 195/65 VR 15 tyres on 'S' models

6J x 15 alloy wheels with 195/65 VR 15 tyres on V6 saloon models

6J x 15 alloy wheels with 205/60 VR 15 tyres on Vitesse

Kerb weight

2.866lb (1,300kg)	820 Fastback
2,944lb (1,335kg)	820e Fastback
2,988lb (1,355kg)	820Se Fastback
2,933lb (1,330kg)	820i Fastback
2,977lb (1,350kg)	820Si Fastback
3,098lb (1,405kg)	827Si Fastback
3,142lb (1,425kg)	Vitesse Fastback
3,241lb (1,470kg)	825D Turbo

Add 34lb (15kg) in each case for automatic gearbox

PERFORMANCE AND FUEL CONSUMPTION FIGURES – 1990–1991 MODELS

These figures are the ones claimed by the manufacturer, except for the 825D fuel consumption figure, which has been calculated.

	0–60mph	Maximum speed	Fuel consumption
820 Fastback manual	11.6sec	112mph (180km/h)	34.8mpg (8.1ltr/100km)
820 Fastback automatic	13.5sec	110mph (177km/h)	33.3mpg (8.5ltr/100km)
820e and Se manual	10.5sec	120mph (193km/h) Fastback	
		119mph (191km/h) Saloon	35.3mpg (8ltr/100km)
820e and Se automatic	11.9sec	118mph (190km/h) Fastback	
		117mph (188km/h) Saloon	31.9mpg (8.9ltr/100km)
820i and Si manual	9.2sec	127mph (204km/h) Fastback	
		126mph (202km/h) Saloon	33.9mpg (8.3ltr/100km)
825D and 825SD Turbo	10.5sec	118mph (190km/h)	45mpg (6.3ltr/100km)
827Si manual	7.6sec	138mph (222km/h) Fastback	
		137mph (220km/h) Saloon	29.6mpg (9.6ltr/100km)
827Si automatic	8.7sec	134mph (215km/h)	27.5mpg (10.3ltr/100km)
Sterling automatic	8.7sec	134mph (215km/h)	27.5mpg (10.3ltr/100km)
Vitesse manual	7.6sec	140mph (225km/h)	29.6mpg (9.6ltr/100km)
Vitesse automatic	8.5sec	135mph (217km/h)	27.5mpg (10.3ltr/100km)

CHAPTER FIVE

STERLING: THE NORTH AMERICAN ADVENTURE

Getting back into what was then the world's largest car market was an important business target for Austin Rover. The British marques whose heritage it embodied had last been sold there in 1981, when the MGB and Triumph TR7 sports cars had ended production without replacements. Austin had not figured there since the 1960s, as its products were just not right for US customers. As for Rover, it had already failed there twice. Its P6 models had been pulled out of the market in 1971, after a determined push in the 1960s, and the SD1 had failed ignominiously in 1981 after just two years of desultory sales.

The problems had been many and various. Insufficient dealers had been one issue, obliging owners to travel sometimes hundreds of miles for parts and servicing. Poor quality had been another – sadly, a typically British disease at the time. And supply had been a third. US buyers were used to walking into a showroom and buying the car they saw there; waiting three months while the car they wanted was built to order was simply not the American way.

So Austin Rover had some big hurdles to overcome, but they believed they could come good with the XX. They were convinced that they could deal with the quality and supply issues. They needed the expansion of sales that the US market could bring, and hoped it would lead on to greater things. 'The United States market is the major export opportunity in Austin Rover's sales-led programme to secure its future growth and prosperity,' said chairman Harold Musgrove.

Meanwhile, in a separately managed operation, Land Rover was also preparing to re-enter the USA (after pulling out in 1974) with its Range Rover. Both Austin Rover and Land Rover saw 1987 as the target date for restarting sales on the far side of the Atlantic. Fortunately, the two brands were not in direct competition with one another, and their endeavours would have very different outcomes.

ESTABLISHING A DEALER NETWORK

The biggest issue for Austin Rover was to set up a dealer network, and plans were being made during 1984. Austin Rover management considered three options: establishing a sole Austin Rover venture, appointing an importer, or embarking on a joint venture with another company. The last of these emerged as the favourite option, and at a press conference held in New York on 9 and 10 May 1985 it was announced that Austin Rover was setting up a joint company with Norman Braman, who owned one of the largest automotive retail chains in the USA. This was Braman Enterprises, headquartered in Florida. The new company would be called Austin Rover Cars of North America, or ARCONA for short. It would have its headquarters in Miami and would be owned 51 per cent by Braman and 49 per cent by Austin Rover. Ray Ketchledge had been appointed as president, coming from Volkswagen of America where he had been corporate marketing director.

Harold Musgrove spoke at that press conference of excellent results with the 800 at customer clinics in the USA. 'The next stage,' he said, 'was to involve Norman Braman 'in key market research to resolve questions such as marque naming'. Braman's first task, however, was to establish a dealer network, and he aimed to appoint as many as 100 dealers in key target areas across the USA. Austin Rover aimed to sell 20,000 of the new Rover in the first year of US sales, and saw huge potential to build on this; a figure of 40,000 a year was mentioned as being achievable, and soon. According to Trevor Taylor, Austin Rover's director of sales and marketing, 'We are going to be very upmarket and very stylish, as Porsche and BMW are in Britain.'

ARCONA favoured moody publicity pictures of the Sterling in the beginning, conveying an upmarket and stylish image. These were the 1987 (left) and 1988 (above) Sterling sales brochures for the USA.

A key event was held at the Marriott O'Hare Hotel in Chicago during June 1985. By that stage, some sixty dealers had expressed an interest in holding franchises, and Norman Braman set up a convention to introduce them – and other potential dealers – to the new cars. No fewer than 1,500 dealers applied for the 850 guest places, and eventually 1,100 guests attended; three meetings were held to accommodate this high level of interest, instead of the planned two. 'We've never known anything like it,' said Norman Braman afterwards. 'We'll have to revise our forecast figures. Originally, we'd planned to import 20,000 cars in the first year. Now we think perhaps we should take more.' Reports spoke of spontaneous applause from the guests when samples of the new car were revealed.

It all seemed to be a huge success. Shortly after the Chicago convention, a meeting of the eighty dealers by then appointed estimated sales of 23,000 cars a year, plus more than 4,700 more if a two-door coupé was added to the range. The original plan had been to appoint dealers in metropolitan New York, on the eastern seaboard and on the West Coast – all areas where there were plenty of young and moneyed new-generation buyers who saw cachet in imported European cars. After this dealer meeting, ARG began to think about extending the dealer network from day one to include Indianapolis, Oklahoma City, Salt Lake City and Birmingham (Alabama).

THE STERLING BRAND

By August 1985, the XX still had no name for the US market, although work had been going on to find the right one for some months. ARG knew that the Rover name would never work: there were still too many potential US customers who had bitter memories of the last cars bearing that name.

At the time of that New York press conference in May 1985, there were twenty names being researched through customer clinics. According to ARG's director of export sales, Peter Johnson, these included Austin Rover 'and some from the past', but it was likely that a completely new name would be chosen.

That was exactly what happened. Some time in late 1985 or early 1986, Austin Rover chose to brand the XX as a Sterling for North America. The name had positive connotations, suggesting both high quality and the British currency of the pound sterling. Interestingly, Honda also decided to market its HX car with a new brand name in the USA, resulting in it becoming the Acura Legend when it went on sale there in 1987. As for the Sterling name, that would also be used to designate the top models of the XX range in other markets. Once the name was announced to the US press, which was probably around the time of the car's launch for other markets in June 1986, a row broke out. The Sterling name was already in use in the USA: a US-assembled version of the Carbodies London taxi was being marketed as a Sterling Limousine. One way or another, though, the objections were overcome and the Sterling name went ahead.

THE US MODELS

The car sold in the USA as a Sterling was not quite the same as the models sold with Rover badges elsewhere. For a start, it carried special Sterling badges, designed to fit the frame of Rover's Viking ship badge but featuring a lion rampant on a very English-looking red cross. The alloy wheels on top

models had a cross-spoked design unique to the US Sterlings at this stage. Then, of course, US safety and emissions regulations also dictated a number of special features.

On the safety side, the front and rear bumpers were extended by about 2½in (10cm) each to meet crash regulations, which actually raised the drag coefficient to 0.33 from the standard 0.32. The bumper wrap-arounds incorporated side marker lights, and the headlights consisted of two separate units so that either one could be replaced separately, although they fitted into the same spaces as on the standard cars. There was also a high-level third brake light mounted on the parcel shelf just inside the rear window. All these changes met US lighting regulations in force at the time.

The only engine option was the Honda V6, and this had been reworked to meet US exhaust emissions regulations. There was a catalytic converter in the exhaust, and a lower compression ratio along with changes to the ignition and fuel-injection systems to suit the 91-octane unleaded petrol that was then ubiquitous in the USA. As a result, power was

ABOVE LEFT: **The Sterling badge was designed to fit where the Rover badge went on cars for other markets. The lion rampant and the red cross were designed to suggest 'Englishness'.**

ABOVE RIGHT: **The badge was repeated on the wheel trims, again in the location normally occupied by the Rover badge.**

LEFT: **This collection of Sterling identification logos was put together by Adrian Chandler.**

AN UNFULFILLED PLAN

The US market's push towards more and more passive safety features in cars led Austin Rover to experiment with a motorized passive occupant restraint system. This was fitted to a sectioned Sterling that was displayed at Autotech '87, the technical congress held by the Institute of Mechanical Engineers at the NEC in Birmingham during December 1987. No such system ever entered production for the 800.

built by the end of 1987. This was a time of optimism, and Ray Ketchledge was in buoyant mood when he spoke to *Autocar* for their issue dated 22 October 1986. The Acura Legend was just going on sale in the USA, but of the Sterling, Ketchledge said: 'The car is everything the Legend isn't. It has warmth, personality and character – it's an underpriced Jaguar.'

Ketchledge also looked forward to expanding the Sterling range:

> *We could sell a convertible easily, but that would be built in the USA off the coupé – it's the only way to do it. Austin Rover is going to give us a decision on the coupé soon and we'll get the hatchback. We can do very well from the derivatives off the XX platform – and we're having input into the YY mid-range car for a Sterling version of that.*

down from the 173bhp of the Rover-badged cars to 151bhp at 5,800rpm. Torque was the same 160lb ft but the peak was generated at a lower 4,500rpm. Although the original plan had been to sell only the V6 car in North America, by the autumn of 1986 an engineering programme was under way to develop the 2-litre M16 for the US market as well.

The first demonstration and test cars – 825SL models – were shipped to ARCONA in Miami during September 1986 and full production of Sterlings for North America began at Cowley in November. There were hopes that US Sterlings would account for one in three of every XX being

Sterling kicked off with an aggressive advertising campaign in the USA. The first advertisements read, 'If only the Japanese could build a car like Jaguar. If only the English could build a car like Honda. If only the Germans could build a luxury car people could afford.' The solution, of course, was the Sterling. On 29 November, *Motor* magazine reported that US dealers already had bulging order books and that, as a

Under the bonnet of the first Sterlings was the Honda 2.5-litre V6, although there were minor differences from models for the rest of the world.

Lined up on the dockside, these cars were among the first shipment of Sterlings to leave Southampton for the USA on 19 December 1986.

More cars arriving at Southampton on 19 December 1986. Note the large cardboard protective packaging around the bumpers.

result, Norman Braman was now predicting eventual annual sales of 90,000 Sterlings.

The first 'sales' shipment of 900 Sterlings, worth £15 million according to an Austin Rover press release at the time, sailed from Southampton on board the *Don Juan* on 19 December, for unloading at New York and Los Angeles. By that time, the US dealer network consisted of 150 outlets, chosen from over 1,200 applicants. Sterlings became available through US showrooms in January 1987, and by then more than 2,000 cars had left Britain for the USA. ARCONA had ordered a minimum of 27,000 Sterlings to be delivered during 1987.

There were two models in the beginning. The entry-level car, the Sterling 825S, was based on the Rover 825i. Priced at US$19,000, this came with a manual gearbox, although in practice most customers ordered the extra-cost automatic – only about 3 per cent of Sterlings for the USA had manual gearboxes. There were steel wheels with plastic trims bearing the Sterling badge, but again alloys could be had at extra cost. Electric seats and air conditioning were both standard.

The more expensive model, at US$25,500, was the Sterling 825SL, which was based on the Rover 825 Sterling. It came with automatic transmission as standard, alloy wheels,

ABS and metallic paint with a contrasting lower body colour. On the inside, the SL had leather upholstery, power-adjustable seats with position memory, an eight-speaker radio-cassette system, a trip computer, a heated driver's seat and a taller console with centre armrest. The alloy wheels had a cross-spoke pattern that was not available on 800s for other markets at the time, but would later became standard on the 800 Sterling models outside the USA.

PRESS REACTIONS

When *Road & Track* magazine tested a Sterling for its May 1987 issue, one of its big concerns was with the differences between the British-built car and the Acura Legend, which had already been on sale in the USA for several months. In the end, it concluded that there were many differences, and that the balance was very much in favour of the Sterling except in two areas. These were the transmission, where the gear-change points seemed to be less happy than in the Legend, and the secondary controls, which were neither intuitive nor easy to use. 'Ergonomically,' they concluded, 'it's a bit of a muddle.'

The real problem with the transmission, however, was the peaky nature of the Honda engine – the very same problem that had become apparent on UK-market cars. 'This engine … has characteristics that make it a fundamentally unhappy powerplant in a luxury sedan,' they stated. Low-end torque was poor, and all the power was at the top end. 'Off the line, the Sterling automatic shifted from 1st to 2nd too soon, immediately dropping the engine back into the torque-void again.' The same shortcoming was apparent on hills:

> Climbing even average grades, both automatics – the Sterling's and the Legend's – struggle noticeably against the poor torque curve. Ascending in high gear at cruising speed, the revs begin to drop, whereupon the transmission kicks down-up-down again, hunting high and low for the right gear and the right engine speed to suit the job.

Rear badging featured the Sterling name on the left and derivative badging on the right.

Road & Track liked the look of the car, finding it very Honda-like from the front but wholly individual from the side. 'Its appearance is sturdy, competent, pleasing – though in this day of increasingly demonstrative luxury sedan design, we find it a trifle unexciting … understated to a fault.' On the road, though, they had few reservations. The steering had a 'businesslike firmness' despite a 'slightly dead feel', and overall 'the combination of steering and handling in the Sterling was absolutely first-rate'. It 'blew the Legend into the weeds on the slalom course', and on braking it outperformed the Legend, which was not yet available with ABS. On the Sterling, 'the brake system is a particularly happy blend'.

Suspension came in for particular praise. There was:

> a sharp, vigorously alert feel to the Sterling's front suspension, a quickness to relay road information that encourages you to go ahead. … Over most potholes and irregularities the suspension showed excellent poise – and then, suddenly, the car would take a terrible bash from some obstacle that seemed no worse than the others. Wheel control was good most of the time, but in just the right – we should say, wrong – circumstances, that odd bump in the road exposes a marked lacked of jounce control, especially at the front.

A moody publicity photo of the Sterling. Clearly visible are the two-piece headlamps and side marker lights, in each case required by **US** legislation.

Inside the Sterling, luxury and high levels of equipment greeted the driver.

Publicity pictures like this suggested that the Sterling was rather more of a sports saloon than its designers had intended.

Lastly, there were a few niggles, both of design (the gearshift prevented the ashtray from opening when in Park) and of execution (the inner door handle frames did not fit properly).

STERLING ON SALE

In the beginning, sales went well. An *Autocar* report on 17 June 1987 noted that sales were right on target and had totalled 4,199 cars in the first three months. There were signs of problems, though. *Road & Track* magazine had been generally well-disposed towards the car, but several of the test cars that the magazine tried had niggling faults, especially electrical ones. 'These little failures are apparently not isolated cases,' reported *Autocar,* 'though they could be just start-up stumbles with a brand new distribution network dealing with a brand new car.' The US dealers, however, were pleased. About 32 per cent of Sterling dealers also sold Cadillacs, and many found the two brands complemented each other's appeal very well.

Nevertheless, US sales in the Sterling's first year fell well short of the predicted 20–23,000, with a total of 14,171. There were two main reasons. First, ARCONA had underestimated demand for the more expensive 825SL models and was caught with the wrong model mix in its showrooms. Second, the word was clearly getting out that the Sterling could be just as unreliable as British cars of old, and unreliability is one thing that US customers will not forgive. A headline-grabbing failing was that the leather upholstery turned green in the sun. The influential J. D. Power customer-satisfaction survey highlighted poor build quality with electrical, paint-work and corrosion problems, and the Sterling dropped to the bottom of the survey's rankings. Meanwhile, the Acura Legend had gone straight to the top in its first year on sale in the USA. As a background to these problems, a strong British currency and a weak dollar meant that Austin Rover were starting to lose money on the venture.

For 1988, ARCONA revised its sales target to a more realistic 17,000 cars. But Sterling sales during 1988 dropped alarmingly, finishing with a year-end total of under 9,000. By May, ARG had decided to take the North American operation back under its own wing; that month, Ray Ketchledge left ARCONA and ARG's Ian Strachan told *Autocar* for that magazine's 25 May issue, 'We're just waiting for the report from the European Commission and the vote of the British Aerospace shareholders before we go ahead.' (ARG had in the meantime been passed into the care of British Aerospace – *see* Chapter 3.)

Although the 1989-model cars that followed that summer had the improved 2.7-litre V6 engine, added a hatchback derivative badged as an 827SLi, and included an SL Limited special edition, sales continued to slide. While Austin Rover tried hard to rectify problems, the verdict on ARCONA was rather more damning. *British Car* magazine noted in a December 1992 retrospective that the Miami operation 'was less than perceptive in understanding what the problems were and how to rectify them. Customer service was inefficient to say the least.'

END OF THE ROAD

Whatever the reasons, sales were now in free fall. ARCONA was finally disbanded in February 1989, and Austin Rover appointed Graham Morris as president of the newly renamed Sterling Motor Cars, which was wholly under ARG control. The base-model 825S was discontinued that summer for the 1990 model year, but sales totals were lower again, despite the lure of a 350-strong Oxford Edition, based on the 827SL and finished in Nordic Blue with additional leather trim items.

By early 1991, there seems to have been optimistic talk of a relaunch, probably focusing on the new R17 models, and to be backed up by the introduction of the new coupé derivative in about June 1992. Austin Rover sources, cited

Fastbacks reached the USA, too. This is a late-model Sterling 827SLi with the unbadged early version of the Roversport alloy wheels.

This was supposedly the last Sterling delivered in the USA. It did time as a press demonstrator and was then bought by a journalist. Like all the later models, it had one-piece headlamps.

in *Car* magazine for March 1991, expected the Rover name and badge to replace Sterling; apparently the thinking was that the success of the Range Rover had lent new credibility to the Rover name in the USA.

However, that was not the scenario that Sally Eastwood encountered when she was asked to take up a new two-year post in Miami, beginning that May. She had been working in human resources for ARG in the UK, and was anticipating a similar job at Sterling's headquarters. But as she explained in April 2012:

> When I got on the plane to go to Miami, I was handed a binder by my senior HR colleague and told that the job was to help close Sterling. In that binder was everything related to Sterling's demise: sales numbers, quality issues, customer dissatisfaction, you name it, along with a timing plan for planning the communication of the closure with employees, dealers, customers and the advertising agency.
>
> So, I arrived in May 1991, and worked with the President of the company (Graham Morris) and the

General Counsel Louis Tertocha, as well as Charlie Hughes at RRONA [Range Rover of North America], in secret for almost three months while we put the plans together for the closure. At the same time, my 'day job' was to be the HR person for Sterling.

> On August 9, 1991 (I will never forget that day) we called an all-employee meeting and at the same time, Graham [Morris] called the advertising agency, and [sent] a communication to all the dealers. At the employee meeting, the slides spoke the story of the company's demise. It was pretty obvious what was coming, and I spoke to every employee individually with a letter and a severance plan for each of them. Obviously sales and marketing staff were let go immediately, with severance, since there was no more to sell or market. All other employees were offered contracts for anywhere between six and twenty-four months, depending on their roles.

So that was the end of the Sterling operation. In five years, 35,700 Sterlings had been built for the US market, as against predictions of more than 20,000 a year, and rising. However, US Sterling owners were not left without any support, as Sally Eastwood remembers:

> We needed to keep a cadre of service, warranty, parts and customer service employees to take care of the vehicles out there in the overall car parc, and assuage customers as much as possible. Some of these employees would leave when the Miami operation closed, and others were offered eventual relocation up to Maryland to be part of RRONA [which became Land Rover of North America – LRNA – in autumn 1992].

Fifteen or twenty former Sterling employees went to Maryland in mid-1992, among them Sally herself. 'Even today [2012],' she says, 'there are ex-Sterling employees who are still at Land Rover' – which of course has since moved its US headquarters three times, first to New Jersey under BMW, then to California under Ford, and back to New Jersey under Tata.

> In that sense, looking after customers and the dealers was very serious. Every effort was made to keep parts in stock and to help dealers fix cars for quite a long period of time – well over five years, from memory, until parts were eventually given to a third party to handle.

Even so, many Sterling owners preferred to get their cars maintained at Acura dealerships, and commonality of mechanical items with the Legend encouraged this.

What is perhaps most striking about the US Sterling episode, however, was its long-term impact on Austin Rover. In the beginning, the company had seen the US market as its biggest export opportunity, one that it had to embrace in order to ensure its long-term prosperity. The Sterling was supposed to be a first step on the ladder, but the car's failure now made it more or less impossible for Austin Rover to become established in North America. If the Sterling had been the success it was originally predicted to be, the chances are that the eventual fate of ARG and its Rover Group successor would have been very different.

STERLING PRODUCTION FIGURES

Manual transmission fitted to 3 per cent (about 1,150).

	S	SL	Si	SLi	Total
1987	8,503	5,668			14,171
1988	5,339	3,560			8,899
1989	881	4,109		881	5,871
1990		2,811	578	602	4,015
1991		1,920	412	412	2,744
Total					**35,700**

THE T16 ENGINE

The 4-cylinder petrol engines accounted for more than half the sales of Rover 800 models, and company car taxation changes in the UK were already increasing the importance of that sector of the executive-car market. So Rover Group engineers put considerable effort into developing the existing M16 engines to keep them fully competitive. The new engine that was announced for the R17 versions of the Rover 800 was called the T16.

The T16 engine shared its bore and stroke dimensions with the M16 engine and with the O-series 2-valve engine that had preceded it. However, it was very far from being a warmed-over M16. Although it shared that engine's basic architecture, all of its components were in fact new.

The M16 engine used a series of external pipes to allow gases to circulate, but the T16 dispensed with these. Instead, channels were cast into block and cylinder head, leaving fewer critical joints to leak and tidying up the external appearance of the engine – an increasingly important factor at the time. The new cylinder head was simpler to manufacture than the M-series type, and there were new cam profiles, which drew on work done for the latest K-series engines that had been introduced in 1988. There were new lightweight pistons and the crankshaft had eight counterweights rather than the four used on the M-series engines, so improving refinement.

Developed from the earlier M16 engine, this was the T16 4-cylinder engine used in the facelifted cars.

A quite remarkable change was made in the belt drive for the camshafts, which now had a semi-automatic tensioner and no longer drove the water pump. Cam belts were expected to last for 100,000 miles (160,000km) between changes as a result. The water pump was now paired with the power steering pump and was mounted externally with it, and the two were driven by the auxiliary drive belt.

The T16 also used Rover's latest MEMS electronic control unit. MEMS stood for Modular Engine Management System, the modular element allowing multiple optional modules to be added to the common hardware core. It had been designed by Rover and Motorola for maximum flexibility to suit both multiple versions of the same engine and completely new engines. Consisting of a single microprocessor that controlled all major engine functions, MEMS could be interrogated simply during a service and recorded faults for future diagnosis. The first production version (MEMS 1.2) appeared in the Austin Montego 2-litre in 1989; the version used in the new T16 engine was MEMS 1.3, modified for use with a catalytic converter.

A very noticeable difference between the T16 and M16 engines in practice was that the newer one had far superior torque characteristics. The figures make that difference very clear: where the M16 developed peak torque of 175Nm (129lb ft) at a high 4,500rpm, the T16 developed 185Nm (136lb ft) at just 2,500rpm, which was well within the most commonly used speed band of the engine. The major change that had made this possible was a new long-tract inlet system, which increased the ram-air effect. A comparison of the paper figures released by Rover suggests otherwise, but in fact the T16 also delivered more top-end power than the M16 when both were fitted with a catalytic converter in the exhaust.

The Exterior Facelift

The budget for the exterior facelift was limited, too, and Ian Elliott remembers one particular limitation that affected what Gordon Sked's designers were able to do.

> There was a stipulation at the outset that the XX doors would have to be carried over without change, which dictated the profiles and crease lines on the flanks (though the plant-on rubbing-strips were reconfigured to disguise this to some extent). When it actually came to tooling the R17 panels, the manufacturing folk put their hands up to say that the XX door tooling was becoming too worn and would have to be replaced.

Not surprisingly, the designers were extremely annoyed, and pointed out that they could have made more radical changes if they had not been constrained by the old door profile. Even so, the new 800 design was a vast improvement over the old. Where the XX tended to look as if the body panels had been shrunk-fit over the inner structure, the R17/R18 design was altogether more rounded and more imposing to look at. Central to the new shape was a proper radiator grille, which replaced the anonymous-looking slot of the original design. This was based on the grille shapes of the much-liked Rover P4 and Rover P5 models of the 1950s and 1960s, which epitomized the Rover image for much of the buying public in the 1990s.

Ian Elliott was then working in the marketing department and had close links with the Rover Sports Register enthusiasts' club. He remembers being asked to borrow a P4 from a club member and deliver it to the design studio for the designers to examine. Later, when he wrote the press pack

The new Rover grille was deliberately designed to recall the 'classic' Rover grille. Here, a Sterling is pictured with the 1973 Rover 3.5-litre (P5B model) that had once been used by Her Majesty the Queen for personal transport.

for the 1992-model 800s, he explained that the new grille combined 'a fully up-to-date, modern style with the degree of heritage and implied quality that an appropriate grille theme can deliver'. The message was underpinned visually by a press photograph showing the revised 800 with a late-model P5 (actually a V8-engined P5B).

With the new grille came a new bonnet panel, new wings and wrap-around front indicator lamps that were supposedly intended to recall those on the 800's hugely stylish predecessor, the Rover SD1. (These, in turn, had

been inspired by their counterparts on the 1968 Ferrari 365 GTB/4 'Daytona'.)

The old doors were disguised by new rubbing-strips, but the back of the car was extensively redesigned. On the R18 saloons, a small window was retained in the rear pillar behind the door, while the rear screen was completely new. The rear wings followed the fuller lines of the front wings and the line of the boot was higher, featuring a new boot-lid panel. On the R17 Fastbacks, the rear quarter-panels were redesigned to suit the overall shape, and there was a new

This is the rear view of the same 1992-model Sterling saloon. The facelifted design certainly made the 800 look more substantial than it had before.

This is an entry-level 820 Si Fastback, the least expensive of the new Rovers. The new style of tail badging is in evidence.

The most obvious exterior differences between entry-level models and the top-model Sterling were the steel wheels with polycarbonate trims (instead of the Sterling's alloy wheels) and the dummy air vents (which replaced the fog lamps that came as standard on the Sterling).

This was the 1992-model SL saloon specification, with attractive six-spoke alloy wheels.

The Vitesse in Fastback form had another new wheel design, this time with seven spokes. This photograph was taken to emphasize the wedge-shape of the car, not always so apparent.

The Vitesse was now available as a saloon as well. The 'Directors Only' parking sign makes its point in this publicity picture.

91

There was a new style of tail badge, seen here on the Vitesse. This example has the optional five-spoke Roversport alloy wheels.

tailgate lower panel. Both models had new and more distinguished tail lights, new bumpers and new rear badges, this time without the Rover name on the left of the boot lid or tailgate.

Then there were new wheel designs, as of course there had to be. For models with steel wheels, the polycarbonate trims were drawn up with a multi-spoked outer ring. For the Sterling, there was a new alloy wheel design with spoked outer ring called Prestige, and the Vitesse came with the five-spoke Roversport alloys that had been previewed on the 820 Turbo 16v, though now with centre badges.

There was no new body kit for the facelifted cars. However, the Vitesse did come with a new rear spoiler that was rigid enough not to need a central support strut. As for the aerodynamics, the drag coefficient for all new Rover 800s, saloons and Fastbacks alike, was quoted as 0.31 – a very competitive figure for its time.

The Inside Story

The theme of harking back to 'traditional' Rovers inspired much of the interior facelift as well. Gordon Sked's designers gave the instrument panel new wood trims, as well as the extra switches needed to operate additional equipment.

The wood finishers throughout the car featured walnut in a wood-aluminium veneer sandwich. The supplier provided sets for each car with a consistent matched colour and conforming to one of eight agreed grain patterns. This was expected to make replacement of a damaged item simpler in service.

On the SLi, Vitesse and Sterling, a traditional analogue clock was chosen for the centre stack, although other models retained a digital type. There were a new steering wheel, derived from the award-winning Safety Wheel (with airbag) introduced on the R8 models, and new steering-column stalks similar to those on the R8. The original Maestro-derived main instrument dials were changed for a new style, and the oil pressure gauge and voltmeter were deleted from the complement of auxiliary gauges. All ICE systems now featured security coding, and most 800 models came with an R652 electronic stereo radio-cassette head unit with cassette auto-reverse and six speakers. An R682 head unit with RDS (Radio Data System) was standard on the Vitesse and optional for most other models, while a system with a six-disc CD autochanger (located in the boot) was standard for the Sterling and optional on other models.

Bigger door bins accommodated more oddments than before. Between the front seats was a new and better integrated floor console, and the electric seat controls had been

The Vitesse came with a new design of cloth trim, although the seats still had leather bolsters.

The facia was recognizably derived from the one that had gone before, but there were subtle changes to make it look more upmarket. The analogue clock in the centre stack was one of them. The steering wheel here contains an airbag.

moved from here to the outboard valances of the seats themselves. The seats, too, were redesigned to give a more luxurious appearance, and for the front of the Vitesse models Sked's team used Recaro sports seats with larger side bolsters and a special Silverstone upholstery fabric. There was a new selection of interior fabrics and colours, too.

Both saloon and Fastback derivatives now had a useful 60/40 split-folding rear seat, which helped with the carrying of long loads. Finally, the saloons came with ICE speakers neatly integrated into the rear parcel shelf.

ABOVE RIGHT: **Clear in this interior picture of the facelifted Vitesse is the Recaro brand name emblazoned across the backs of the seats.**

RIGHT: **The effect of all that wood and leather is clear in this picture of the Sterling's front compartment. There was no doubting that this was a luxury car.**

What Rover had done, though, it had done well. 'The softer-styled bodywork ... has clear aspirations: executive status. Worthy and capable as it was, the old Rover 800's paper-edge shape never did.' The interior came in for praise, too: 'one of the Sterling's most appealing aspects is its opulent cabin', although there was only 'adequate, but by no means exceptional leg and headroom front and rear'. The magazine found that 'noise suppression is excellent: the Sterling is exceptionally refined at speed'. Even the build quality was very good:

> *Inside, the quality element can't quite match some of the German competition, but the test car's exterior finish and panel fit are as good as you'll find for the money.*

Awards and Changes

The Association of British Insurers (ABI) was working towards the introduction of a simplified car insurance system during 1992, under which every model would be allocated to one of twenty groups on which insurance premiums would be based. On 15 April, Rover were able to announce the good news that the ABI had given the 800 range the lowest overall group rating of any executive-car range, and that some models were rated several groups lower than their direct rivals from other manufacturers. There was further good news on 3 June, when the BVLRA announced that the 800 range had won its 1991 Anti-Theft Award (which was always awarded retrospectively).

Meanwhile, there had been a public outcry about the 'on the road' packages used by Rover and some other makes in Britain to inflate the showroom price above that listed for the car. Rover's response was to remove these charges and to lower prices for the 800 range as well. So from 17 April 1992, the 800 prices inclusive of taxes became:

820i	£16,750
820Si	£18,450
825D	£18,495
Vitesse	£19,845
825SD	£20,185
820SLi	£20,195
825SLD	£22,345
827Si	£22,585
827SLi	£24,745
Sterling	£26,895

The wheels say **SLi** but the fog lights say **Sterling** ... by juggling options, it was possible to create a car with a specification almost unrecognizable to anybody but an 800 aficionado – or a Rover salesman.

While all this was happening, the range was not standing still. The diesel and Vitesse models went on sale in February 1992, as planned, and when the Geneva Motor Show opened on 3 March Rover revealed its new 800 Coupé. This was to be built only with the Honda V6 engine. The car was not yet available but would go on sale in June at a price that made it far and away the most expensive 800 derivative. The showroom price was £30,770, and the only cost option available was a driver's side airbag at £725. (See Chapter 8 for the full story of the Coupé, which, sadly, became an elegant failure.)

There was more news on 20 July, when the Rt Hon. Michael Heseltine, president of the Board of Trade, formally opened a new assembly hall at Rover's Cowley works. Built alongside the existing paint plant at a cost of £200 million, it had been designed to allow all car manufacturing operations at Cowley to be carried out on a single site; until then, there had been three separate factories. The 800 had been assembled in the old North Works but would now move to the new assembly hall – the old North and South Works would close at the end of 1992 and be sold off to create a new business and industrial park.

success in itself but not quite as exciting as it sounded in view of the generally disappointing sales of the range. (It was also selected as Best Executive Car in the 1994 Fleet News Awards.)

One important upgrade was made in December 1993, when a driver's side airbag was standardized on all models. The cost of this was absorbed shortly afterwards in some price increases that took effect on 20 December. There were increases right across the Rover range, averaging 2.9 per cent, which left the UK price list looking like this (inclusive of all taxes):

820i	£17,495
825D	£18,895
820Si	£19,495
Vitesse	£20,495
825SD	£20,995
820SLi	£21,195
825SLD	£22,695
827Si	£23,495
827SLi	£25,195
Sterling	£27,995
Coupé	£29,995

The 1993 and 1994 Model Years

Rover's energies were diverted elsewhere for the 1993 model year, at the end of which the new 600 model would be announced to fill the gap in the company's model ranges between the 400 and the 800. There were no significant changes for the 1993 models, and colours and trims remained unchanged. So did specifications, although radio aerials now disappeared from top models, which took on full diversity antennae that used the electrical elements of the heated rear window as an aerial. Of course, no year could go by without Rover increasing its prices at least once, and there was a general price increase across the whole range on 21 December 1992.

There were no major changes to the 800 range for the 1994 model year. Rover's flagship range was at this stage the best-selling executive car in Britain – a

This 1994 825SD was available for journalists to try at the annual SMMT Test Day at Millbrook that year – so the author did, and took a brief break to photograph the car as well.

LEFT: **This press photo of an SL-specification Fastback was issued in February 1994. It could have been an 820SLi, an 827SLi or even an 825SLD; there was no way of telling from this angle.**

BELOW: **This rather effective publicity picture shows the capacious boot and the transverse engine of an 820SLi from the 1994 model year. By that stage, the sunroof was standard.**

TAX-BREAKERS – THE ROVER 820 AND 820SE

The UK government made a number of changes to taxation on company cars with effect from 6 April 1994. Rover capitalized on this by introducing two new models with limited availability. These were the Rover 820, priced at £14,995, and the Rover 820SE, priced at £16,495. Both were available as either Fastback or saloon, and both had the 136PS (134bhp) T16 engine, the five-speed manual gearbox and six-spoke alloy wheels. All ten of the colours available for standard 800s could be had, with the usual interior colour options. The differences between the two models lay in their equipment levels, with the 820SE boasting ABS, electric rear windows, kerbside illumination, Windsor upholstery (the 820 had Ascot), walnut door fillets, a windscreen shade band and an electric sunroof.

   'If you want the prestige of a Rover 800 combined with the most efficient price for an executive car then talk to your local Rover dealer soon as supplies of these models are limited,' read the sales brochure. It is not clear how many were made or when availability ceased.

CHANGE OF OWNERSHIP – AGAIN

The biggest news of the 1994 model year was not one that affected the Rover product ranges but the announcement in January 1994 that the Rover Group had been sold to the German BMW car company.

British Aerospace had taken ownership of the Rover Group in August 1988, but it had no plans to extend that ownership beyond the five years that were a tacit part of the original agreement with the British government. Honda were asked if they wanted to take a bigger stake in Rover, but they declined. So in late 1993 the word went out – very discreetly, it appears – that BAe would be interested to hear from potential buyers for the car business.

At that stage, BMW was looking to expand under its recently appointed chairman, Bernd Pischetsrieder. It had two choices: it could either expand slowly, by introducing new model ranges one at a time, or take over an existing company that was already selling in areas of the market where BMW was not represented. The Rover Group was a good fit for that second option and towards the end of 1993 there was an increase in the number of visitors from BMW to the Rover Group sites. As there was already a business link between the two companies – Land Rover were using BMW diesel engines in their Range Rover – this did not arouse any undue suspicion within the workforce.

By the end of January 1994 everything had been arranged. An agreement was signed on 29 January, under which BMW would buy from BAe all the shares in Rover Group Holdings Ltd for a price of £800 million. As Rover and Honda UK Manufacturing had cross-holdings amounting to 20 per cent of each company's shares, there was still some tidying up to do. Although BMW was prepared to let the relationship with Honda continue, the Japanese company chose to end its links with Rover and issued a statement to that effect on 21 February. Honda agreed to continue with the supply of components (such as the 800's V6 engine) for the foreseeable future, but Rover now became a wholly owned subsidiary of BMW.

Changes and New Models, May 1994

A number of changes to the 800 range, planned many months before the BMW takeover, took effect in early May 1994. There were two new models in the UK and a number of specification improvements on the existing 800s, without any price increases. An airbag was added for the front passenger, while in saloons the rear passenger sitting in the middle was now protected by a full three-point safety harness. A new engine-immobilizer system was added to the anti-theft measures, which already included remote locking with a rolling code. The manual release levers for boot and fuel filler were replaced by a combined electric release button, now located on the centre console, and an analogue clock was made standard across the range.

The S-level trim now included a burr walnut surround for the ashtray and clock on the centre stack, and both S and SL models gained body-colour door mirrors and the 16in seven-spoke alloy wheels that had previously only been available on the Vitesse. S and SL models also gained the diversity aerial already standard on top models, together with a new R850 ICE head unit incorporating separate bass and treble controls. Front-seat heaters were

standardized with leather upholstery, and there was a new range of colours.

One of the new models was intended specifically for the UK market in order to take advantage of changes in company car taxation. The 827i provided a V6 model that fell into the under-£20,000 category where taxation was lower.

From May 1994, an airbag for the front passenger became available. It was neatly integrated into the dashboard, but the useful parcel shelf was lost in the process.

Again from the 1994 model year, this is the dashboard of a Sterling – although in this case without the passenger's side airbag.

In all important respects its equipment level was the same as that of the 820i but it came with ABS, which was standard on all V6-engined 800s. The second new model announced at this stage was altogether more exciting, and would be available in export markets as well. This was the Vitesse Sport.

The Vitesse Sport

Rover had been gradually working towards the Vitesse Sport since 1991 and the interim-production 820 Turbo 16v (see also Chapter 4). On both this model and the turbocharged Vitesse that followed it, power and torque had to be limited because the standard PG1 gearbox was not strong enough and high torque inputs in a front-wheel-drive car could lead to uncontrollable torque steer.

At long last, Rover had now managed to get an uprated gearbox with shot-peened gears into production. Matching this to a torsen differential – which Rover described as a traction control system but which actually limited the effects of sudden high torque inputs – allowed the outputs of the turbocharged 2-litre engine to be increased. The changes were primarily effected by alterations to the engine management control software, which now permitted peak power of 200PS (197bhp) and maximum torque of 240Nm (177lb ft) at a usefully low 2,000rpm. Even now, the control software gave a very flat torque curve from 3,000rpm upwards, mainly in order to protect the gearbox.

These changes made a big difference to the performance. The Vitesse Sport could hit 60mph from rest in 7.3sec and power on to a top speed of 143mph (230km/h). The

renewed urge was matched by stiffer road springs, which were 20mm lower than before, thicker anti-roll bars both front and rear, and revised steering geometry to give sharper responses. The flatter and beefier torque output was a major factor in contributing to improved fuel economy on the Vitesse Sport, which achieved a composite figure of 34.7mpg (8.2ltr/100km) – more than 11 per cent better than for the standard Vitesse.

The standard Vitesse remained available alongside the Vitesse Sport, which could be had as either a saloon or a Fastback. Visually, the new model could be recognized by its new 17in six-spoke alloy wheels running on low-profile 215/45 ZR 17 tyres, which made their own contribution to its sharp handling. With the two pearlescent paint options, Nightfire Red and Tahiti Blue, and with British Racing Green, the bodyside protection mouldings and bumper tops could be painted in the body colour. However, there were few interior changes. A passenger's side airbag was standard, there were leather grips for the gearshift and handbrake, and a top-quality R950 ICE system was standard.

At the same time, a new interior upgrade option became available for both the Vitesse and the new Vitesse Sport. Known as the Lux pack and priced in the UK at £2,000, it provided automatic temperature control, heated front seats with electric adjustment on the driver's side, and the full-leather trim otherwise seen in the Coupés.

Price Reductions, January and June 1994

Rover had been trying hard to improve its competitiveness by reducing costs. The first news of this was released on 11

With its lowered stance and big six-spoke alloy wheels, the 1995-model Vitesse Sport looked the part more than any earlier Vitesse, although arguably the 1991 820 Turbo ran it a close second.

January 1994, when the company announced a programme of price reductions for servicing, many achieved by altering service schedules so that some renewable components were actually renewed less frequently. The main effect on the 800 range was that the intermediate 6,000-mile service for the 827 models was dropped from the recommended schedule, thus extending service intervals.

After the Budget in early spring changed benefit-in-kind taxation on company cars in the UK so that it was based solely on the purchase price of the vehicle, Rover entered negotiations with their dealers to help drive down prices.

THE TURBOCHARGED T16 ENGINE

The turbocharged T16 engine and its associated drivetrain were not developed purely for the Vitesse Sport. They gave Rover a powertrain that could be used in several different models, and had already appeared two years earlier in the top-model 'Tomcat', the 220 Coupé Turbo. In July 1994 it was then introduced for the 620ti model. The link with the 620ti was exploited in many export markets, where the turbocharged 800 was marketed as a companion 'performance' model under the name of 820ti.

For the 800 range, they were able to agree a reduction in dealer margins to 5 per cent, resulting in a new set of showroom prices effective from 1 June. These were as follows, inclusive of taxes and once again in ascending order:

820i	£15,995
820Si	£17,495
825D	£17,950
Vitesse	£19,450
820SLi	£19,995
825SD	£19,995
827Si	£19,995
Vitesse Sport	£20,995
Vitesse with Lux Pack	£21,495
825SLD	£21,595
827Si	£22,495
Vitesse Sport with Lux pack	£22,795
827SLi	£23,795
Sterling	£25,595
Coupé	£28,495

Vitesse Sport and the Press

'At last Rover has made a winner out of the car that carries its most evocative mantle,' wrote *Autocar & Motor* magazine when it tested a Vitesse Sport for its 27 July 1994 issue.

'And how.' The car proved capable of matching Rover's claim of 7.3sec for the 0–60mph sprint and with a top speed of 142mph (229km/h) on test was within 1mph of the claimed maximum. This was stirring stuff indeed, despite the car's 'relatively disturbing appetite for unleaded' – 19.8mpg (14.3ltr/100km) overall on test. This was far below the maker's claim of 34.7mpg overall; perhaps hard test driving had made much of the difference, but the figure did suggest that the Rover Group figure was optimistic.

Even so, the acceleration was not the most impressive feature of the new car; it was the handling:

> The Vitesse Sport bears about as much resemblance dynamically to its predecessor as that car did to the ... much-missed [SDI] original. ... To call the change in the Vitesse's handling surprising would be a tragic understatement. A small miracle would be more apt. Previously one of the least talented or enjoyable cars of its kind to punt rapidly down a decent road, the traction control-equipped Vitesse Sport is now a car that even the most committed enthusiast would enjoy, with much-improved body control, less torque steer and meatier, more communicative steering.

The improvement had not been achieved at the expense of ride quality, either, which was a 'real head-turner'. Sadly, though, a tendency to fade revealed that the brakes were 'not up to the job of containing the Vitesse's potential'. The pedal also had a disappointingly 'dead' feel.

The performance was not achieved without some sacrifices, though:

> However smoothly its turbo spins or how impressively it performs against the clock, you are rarely in any doubt that there are only four cylinders thrumming away under the Rover's stylish bonnet, not six as there are in most of its rivals. ... Stretch the T16 close to its red line and the combined gruffness of the engine and exhaust notes soon have you wishing for the inherently smoother operations that two extra cylinders would bring.

Overall, 'it would be wrong to think of the Vitesse Sport as a tyre-shredding hot rod; more a genuine fast-cruising executive whose sporting aspirations are a sideline to the main issue.'

The 1995 Model Year

The focus was off the 800 range for the 1995 model year while the Rover Group concentrated on other new models. (In autumn 1994 came the new Range Rover and in March 1995 the second-generation 400 models were launched.) The new Vitesse Sport models had to provide the momentum to keep interest in the range alive for the moment, and a Fastback model was among the cars on the Rover stand at the British International Motor Show in October 1994. It was accompanied by an 820Si saloon, an 825SLD Fastback, a Sterling saloon and an 800 Coupé.

The colour options were changed and there was a reshuffle of colour availability (see table at the end of this chapter). There was also a reduction in the number of wheel styles available, of which there were now just four. Only entry-level models now had steel wheels; the S and SL trim levels now shared seven-spoke alloys with the Vitesse; the Vitesse Sport had six-spoke alloys; and the Sterling and Coupé continued with the Prestige style of alloys.

On 22 December 1994, showroom prices were increased by an average of 1.9 per cent across the Rover range. Inclusive of taxes, they became as follows:

820i	£16,395
820i with ABS	£16,995
820Si	£17,895
825D with ABS	£18,895
Vitesse	£19,995
820SLi	£20,395
825SD	£20,495
827i	£20,495
Vitesse Sport	£21,495
825SLD	£21,995
Vitesse with Lux pack	£21,995
827Si	£22,995
Vitesse Sport with Lux pack	£23,395
827SLi	£24,395
Sterling	£27,495
Coupé	£29,195

The 1995 model year would be a particularly long one as there was no mention of 1996-model 800s until the very start of the 1996 calendar year. Those new models would not disappoint.

PAINT AND TRIM OPTIONS – 1992–1995

1992 and 1993 model years

There were eleven paint options, of which four were solid types, five were metallic and two were pearlescent (micatallic) types. One of the metallics was exclusive to the Sterling. All paints used clear-over-base technology.

There were five interior colours: Granite and Stone Beige with fabric; Light Granite and Light Stone Beige with leather; and Granite with Ash Grey for the Vitesse. Ascot (woven jacquard) fabric was used for the entry-level 820i and 825D models; Windsor (double-needle raschelle velour) fabric was for the Si, SD, SLi and SLD derivatives; Silverstone (woven jacquard) fabric and leather were combined for the Vitesse; and the Sterling had Prestige leather.

PAINT AND TRIM OPTIONS FOR 1992 AND 1993 MODELS

Paint	Availability	Interior
Black	All models	Stone Beige and Light Stone Beige standard; Granite and Light Granite optional; Granite with Ash Grey (Vitesse)
British Racing Green metallic	All models	Stone Beige and Light Stone Beige standard; Granite and Light Granite optional; Granite with Ash Grey (Vitesse)
Caribbean Blue pearlescent	All models	Stone Beige and Light Stone Beige standard; Granite and Light Granite optional; Granite with Ash Grey (Vitesse)
Flame Red	Not Sterling or Coupé	Granite; Granite with Ash Grey (Vitesse)
Midnight Blue	Not Vitesse, Sterling or Coupé	Granite
Nightfire Red pearlescent	All models	Stone Beige and Light Stone Beige standard; Granite and Light Granite optional; Granite with Ash Grey (Vitesse)
Nordic Blue metallic	Not Vitesse	Granite or Light Granite
Quicksilver metallic	Not Vitesse	Granite or Light Granite; Light Stone Beige optional on Coupé only
Storm Grey metallic	Not Vitesse	Granite or Light Granite; Light Stone Beige optional on Coupé only
White Diamond	Not Sterling or Coupé	Granite; Granite with Ash Grey (Vitesse)
White Gold metallic	Sterling and Coupé only	Light Stone Beige

1994 model year

There were eleven paint colours (*see* overleaf), of which four were solid types, five were metallics, and two pearlescents. Sterling and Coupé models were not available in the solid colours.

There were five upholstery types. The entry-level type (820i, 825D and later 827i) was Ascot cloth; next up was Windsor cloth for the S and SL trim levels. There was 'half-leather' with Silverstone cloth and leather bolsters for the Vitesse, and leather as standard for the Sterling; leather was an extra-cost option for the SL models. Finally, the Coupés had 'full leather', where the leather trim was extended to cover additional surfaces such as the dashboard.

Note that Granite and Stone Beige were not available on Sterling or Coupé models, where they were replaced by Light Granite and Light Stone Beige, respectively.

1995 model year

There were eleven paint colours, of which four were solid types, four were metallics, and three pearlescents. Only seven of these colours could be had on the Vitesse and Vitesse Sport models, but otherwise all colours were available on all models and with all trim levels except the Luxury Option Pack (see below). In practice, the new colours for 1995 were announced with the Vitesse Sport models in May 1994.

continued on page 104

TECHNICAL SPECIFICATIONS – 1992–1995 MODELS *(continued)*

Disc brakes all round, with single-cylinder floating calipers; handbrake acting on rear discs
Ventilated front discs with 262mm diameter on 4-cylinder models and 285mm diameter on V6 models
Solid rear discs with 260mm diameter on all models
Two diagonally split hydraulic circuits; ABS standard on Vitesse and optional on all other models except 820

Dimensions

Overall length	192.2in (4,882mm)
Overall width	68.1in (1,730mm)
	76.9in (1,955mm) over mirrors
Overall height	54.8in (1,393mm)
Wheelbase	108.9in (2,766mm)
Front track	58.4in (1,483mm)
Rear track	57.1in (1,450mm)

Wheels and tyres

6J x 15 steel wheels with 195/65 VR 15 tyres on 820i, 820Si, 825D, 825SD and 827Si

6J x 15 six-spoke alloy wheels with 195/65 VR 15 tyres on 820SLi, 825SLD and 827SLi
6J x 15 Prestige alloy wheels with 195/65 VR 15 tyres on Sterling
6J x 16 five-spoke Roversport alloy wheels with 205/55 VR 16 tyres on Vitesse
6J x 17 alloy wheels with 215/45 ZR 17 tyres on Vitesse Sport/820ti

Kerb weight

Figures shown are for saloons; Fastbacks were 66lb (30kg) heavier across the range.

2,944lb (1,335kg)	820i
2,977lb (1,350kg)	820Si
2,998lb (1,360kg)	820SLi
3,075lb (1,395kg)	Vitesse
3,108lb (1,410kg)	827Si
3,130lb (1,420kg)	827SLi
3,175lb (1,440kg)	825D
3,197lb (1,450kg)	825SD
3,219lb (1,460kg)	825SLD and Sterling

PERFORMANCE AND FUEL CONSUMPTION FIGURES – 1992–1995 MODELS

Acceleration and maximum speed figures are the ones claimed by the manufacturer. Fuel consumption is the calculated average of figures for Urban, steady 56mph and steady 75mph cycles. Metric equivalents have been added.

	0–60mph	Maximum speed	Fuel consumption
820i, 820Si and 820SLi manual	9.6sec	125mph (201km/h)	37mpg (7.6ltr/100km)
820i, 820Si and 820SLi automatic	11.7sec	121mph (195km/h)	35mpg (8.1ltr/100km)
825D, 825SD and 825SLD	10.5sec	118mph (190km/h)	45mpg (6.3ltr/100km)
Vitesse	7.9sec	137mph (220km/h)	No figures given
Vitesse Sport	7.3sec	143mph (230km/h)	34.7mpg (8.2ltr/100km)
827Si and 827SLi manual	8.2sec	133mph (214km/h)	31mpg (9.1ltr/100km)
827Si, 827SLi and Sterling automatic	9.0sec	131mph (211km/h)	29mpg (9.8ltr/100km)

CHAPTER SEVEN

THE 1996–1998 MODELS

When the 1996 models were announced on 16 January 1996, they came with the biggest set of changes since the R17 and R18 models had been introduced back in 1991. Rover had combined an engineering package of new powertrains and suspension revisions with a strongly attractive package of features that reinforced the 'traditional' image that Rover were keen to maintain for their flagship model. And most obvious even to a casual onlooker was that the model distinctions were no longer apparent from badges; with the exception of the Sterling and Vitesse variants, every model simply carried an '800' badge on its tail.

The focus in January was on the top models with their new Rover KV6 engines. The 4-cylinder petrol and diesel models did not receive all the associated enhancements until March. That month also brought an additional Coupé model, when a turbocharged 4-cylinder model with the Vitesse's powertrain and suspension joined the range.

For the final three years of Rover 800 production, derivative badges were abandoned and all models carried the same identification at the rear. The smoked tail-light lenses are visible here.

THE KV6 ENGINE

It had become clear to Rover that they would eventually need a new large-capacity petrol engine when Honda had moved to a new V6 for their own cars but had agreed to keep the 2.7-litre V6 in production for Rover's benefit. That need became more urgent when BMW bought Rover in 1994 and Honda distanced itself from the two companies. What was needed was a modern V6 engine that could be used for the final seasons of 800 production and would then go on to power other models in the Rover range. Compact dimensions were important, because the new V6 might be needed for smaller cars with smaller engine bays than that of the Rover 800.

The newest petrol engine range from Rover, the K-series introduced in 1988, had introduced some valuable new design features and it made good sense to incorporate these into the new V6. As a result, the new Rover engine became known as the KV6 type.

The KV6 was drawn up with two different swept volumes, 2 litres and 2.5 litres, although only the larger size was planned for the 800 range. From the 4-cylinder K-series it took the ultra-compact bore spacing and 'damp' liner construction, as well as the combustion chamber and valve train layout. The architecture of the V6 design did not lend itself to the K-series' famous 'sandwich' construction, but the principles of using the compressive strength of aluminium alloy and minimizing tensile loadings were carried over. So was the idea of a bearing 'ladder', which gave additional strength to the crankcase and was known on the KV6 as the bearing 'basket'. The shallow sump, too, was structural. Like the Honda V6 it was to replace, this engine had both block and heads made from aluminium alloy.

Other K-series features carried over to the KV6 were the internal crankcase vents that doubled as oil drain paths and the stainless-steel head gaskets with flame rings around the bores and silicone rubber beads to seal the water and oil

paths effectively. However, this new engine also had some quite remarkable design features of its own.

It was drawn up with four camshafts, rather than the two used on the Honda engine, as this improved its tuneability. The engine's designers were able to minimize its width by avoiding a large camshaft drive wheel on the outboard (exhaust) camshaft of each cylinder bank. Instead, they used a crossover drive with a short rubber belt from the rear of each inlet camshaft to its corresponding exhaust camshaft, thus requiring smaller drive wheels. This arrangement also allowed a shorter and simpler run for the main cam drive belt. A further contribution to the engine's slim profile was that there were no cam cover boxes over the exhaust camshafts, as the breather and oil separation function was catered for within the inlet cam box on each cylinder bank.

Another ingenious feature was an induction system with variable geometry. Quite unlike the Variable Induction System of the Honda engine, this used twin throttles and twin

The arrival of Rover's own 2.5-litre KV6 engine reduced the company's dependence on Honda, although early examples of the engine were rather troublesome. The engine would go on to be used in the Rover 75 (the successor to the 800 range) and the Land Rover Freelander.

This was the crossover drive arrangement that helped to minimize the width of the KV6 engine. The exhaust camshafts are driven by belts from the rear of the inlet camshafts.

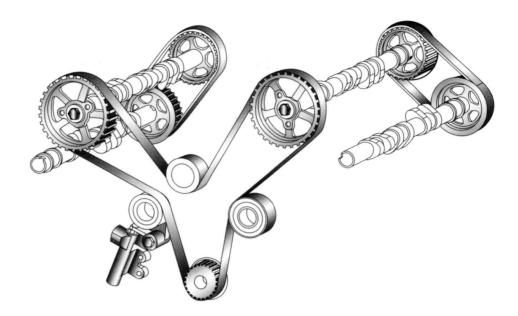

plenums, one serving each bank of three cylinders. The two plenums could be linked through a valve controlled from the engine-management system, and the system was programmed to provide the optimum induction characteristics at all points of the engine's rev range. To the driver, the most noticeable characteristic of this system was the good mid-range torque that it provided.

The KV6 had a three-plane crankshaft with four main bearings, forged steel conrods and lightweight pistons. Fuel was injected sequentially to each cylinder, and there was no distributor; instead, each cylinder had its own dedicated coil, which was fired when needed. The multiple engine control demands were entrusted to the most powerful version yet of Rover's MEMS management system, the 2J type.

The end result was an engine that was the most compact of its type then manufactured, and had exceptionally low weight for its power output. It had more power and better torque than the 2.7-litre Honda engine it was designed to replace, and offered better economy and lower emissions. There was, though, a problem.

Rover anticipated that demand for its new KV6 engine would be limited during the lifetime of the 800 Series. The vast majority of 800s sold were 4-cylinders, and to save both time and investment the KV6 assembly line was set up on a deliberately temporary basis. It was, in effect, a pilot-production line that would be used until new models demanded a greater volume of KV6 engines. The pilot-pro-

duction nature of the operation was reflected by Rover's suppliers, with many early examples of the engine suffering from poor-quality castings. One result was that the KV6 very quickly developed a reputation for blowing its head gaskets – a problem that was not fully eliminated until revised versions of the engine entered production for the Rover 75 in 1998.

This poor early reputation for its new engine did Rover no favours. According to Geoffrey Dudley, in *The Outer Cabinet*, the Government Car Service had some bad experiences with KV6-engined 800s, which made them reluctant to take the similarly engined Rover 75 later – although they did eventually have some on the fleet. (The Government Car Service maintains the fleet of chauffeur-driven cars used by government ministers.)

OTHER POWERTRAIN CHANGES

The 4-Cylinder Engines

It is easy to forget that the KV6 was only one element in the powertrain revisions for the 1996 models, which Rover service literature suggests began at VIN 230967. In fact, all the engines – 2-litre petrol and 2.5-litre turbodiesel – had benefited from engineering changes.

The T16 petrol engines took on a multi-layered steel head gasket, elastomeric cam cover seals and a new version of the MEMS management system (MEMS 1.9) with remapped fuelling to give better response and smoother power delivery. The ignition now incorporated a 'wasted spark' arrangement, firing all four plugs at the same time.

The diesels, meanwhile, now had fully electronic control, which enabled them to meet the lower diesel emissions regulations in force from January 1997 under the ECD2 ('Euro II') regime. A revised combustion chamber design made its contribution to this, while hydraulic tappets and a new engine top cover helped to reduce noise levels. The revised diesel came with more power, and generated its maximum torque at lower speeds, too.

Rover also simplified the choices for performance-oriented drivers by ending production of the 180PS (178bhp) turbocharged T16 engine in the Vitesse and making the 200PS (197bhp) engine the only type available for 1996. The name Vitesse Sport disappeared, too, and the 200PS model was renamed a plain Vitesse.

Gearboxes

The Honda V6 engine had driven through Honda's own four-speed automatic and five-speed manual gearboxes, but Rover aimed to reduce their dependence on the Japanese company as much as possible. So they found a new automatic gearbox for the KV6, a four-speed made by JATCO in Japan and known as the JF403E type. This was one of the latest generation of 'intelligent' gearboxes with electronic control, and it came not only with an integral lock-up clutch to reduce power losses but also with sensors that detected when a downchange would be useful to give overrun braking if the car was travelling downhill. It also had three selectable modes: in addition to Normal, there were the self-explanatory Sport and a Winter mode that locked out first gear and restricted the transmission's use of its lock-up function to prevent wheelspin.

For those who insisted on having a manual gearbox with the KV6, Rover supplied the uprated PG1 five-speed and torsen differential developed for the Vitesse Sport models. There was also a minor change to the gearbox for the diesel models at this stage. A type known to Rover as the T750 replaced the earlier T650 type. Still made by New Venture Gears, it was essentially the same gearbox but appears to have had a larger oil capacity.

With the new engine came a new **JATCO** automatic gearbox. The **PRND321** shift gate was more conventional than the one on the Honda gearbox. To the left of the lever are the selector buttons for **Winter** mode (top) and **Sport** mode.

OTHER CHANGES

The powertrain changes were the headline news on the 1996-model 800s, but there were plenty of other revisions of note. All models gained smoked light lenses, front and rear, along with silver grille vanes in place of the earlier black ones, and chromed tailpipes.

Colour Options

There was an increase in the paint colour options, from 1995's eleven to a total of seventeen. Black was relegated to a special-order option, but four of the six pearlescent colours could be had with a complementary colour below the bump-strip level and a matching coachline. These Duo Tone finishes were strikingly effective but remained fairly rare because, inevitably, they cost extra.

The interior colour options were simplified quite considerably, so that each paint colour came with a 'default' interior trim or the alternative of a universally available Granite grey with Ash piping and carpets; in fact, one colour could be had only with the Granite trim. The mid-range 825Si and 825SLi (the models still existed even though the badges did not) were nevertheless made to feel more luxurious with a new seat fabric known as Saxon that came with contrast piping in a colour specially chosen to complement the exterior paintwork. Separate floor mats for all occupants in a colour to match that piping added to the luxurious feel, and all models now gained a gold 'Rover' inlay on the front door wood inserts.

RIGHT: **The high-performance turbocharged 4-cylinder engine was used in both the Vitesse and, in the foreground here, the Coupé.**

BELOW: **The four Duo Tone options introduced for 1996 were rarely seen.**

Caspian Blue/Aegean

Pearlescent British Racing Green/Willow

Oxford Blue/Ionian

Bolero Red/Pewter

A third brake light, seen here at the bottom of the rear window on a saloon model, was a new feature on the 1996 range. The centre headrest for the rear seat was a new feature, too.

Refinement, Safety and Security

There were also improvements in three other main areas: refinement, safety and security. The cars were now coming up for ten years old, and were beginning to show their age a little in the area of refinement. So a particular aim had been to suppress wind and road noise further. To this end, there were changes to the suspension bushes, the damping and the steering, plus new tyre specifications and better door seals.

Safety was meanwhile addressed by making twin airbags along with front seat-belt pre-tensioners standard on the KV6 models (but not, sadly, the 4-cylinders). The KV6 saloons also gained a central rear head restraint as standard, although the coupés with their two individual rear seats had no need of this and did not get it. A third brake light (sometimes known as a CHMSL – Centre High-Mounted Stop Light) also became standard.

On the security side, the 800s all gained deadlocks activated from the remote locking 'plip' by a rolling code. Passive immobilization was automatically activated when the ignition key was removed, thanks to a transponder located in the ignition lock. For extra anti-theft protection, the car's VIN was etched onto its glass, and locking wheel nuts were made standard.

Finally, although it made little difference in practice, Rover took to describing the three diesel models by new names: 825Di, 825SDi and 825SLDi.

THE KV6 ENGINE AND THE PRESS

There was a huge aura of disappointment about *Autocar*'s road test of a KV6-engine Sterling in its issue dated 21 February 1996. Though they loved the new engine, which they described as 'beltingly good', they concluded that 'until we can experience the KV6 in a car more worthy of its talents, its full potential will remain cloaked by the car that surrounds it'.

Autocar compared the engine with two of the latest V6s from other makers, the Ecotec V6 in the Vauxhall Omega and the Duratec V6 in the Ford Mondeo. They found the Rover KV6 to be the smoothest of the three, but lamented that 'a sportier exhaust note would ram home its power advantage'. Even so:

the engine sounds and feels right [and] you need do no more than glance at the power and torque graphs ... to see how impressively this [variable induction system] works against its chief rivals from Ford and Vauxhall.

The new engine was economical, too:

the fuel returns of the KV6 are ... impressive, with an overall economy of 24.6mpg compared to the 19mpg realized by the outgoing Honda-engined Sterling. Using a cautious right foot, you should expect upwards of 32mpg.

The problem was that the 800 itself was now feeling and looking old. The *Autocar* summary of negative points in its test focused entirely on the host car; they listed 'ageing design, terrible ride over bumps, dull handling, messy switchgear, dated appearance' as the stand-out features. Clearly, they felt the car was past its sell-by date.

PRICING AND SPECIAL ORDERS

There had been a lot of discussion in the media about unfair pricing of cars, with various essential additions not being

The overall appearance of the 800 range did not change for the 1996 season. This is a KV6 model, either an 825Si or an 825SLi – both looked the same from outside. It was photographed at Blenheim Palace in Oxfordshire.

included in the price advertised in showrooms. So Rover Group decided to tackle this with what they called 'no-nonsense' pricing that became effective on 3 June 1996. Prices from that date included VAT, number plates, twelve months' road tax (which was then charged at a flat rate of £140 on all cars) and servicing up to (but not including) 12,000 miles or twelve months. So the new range of prices in the UK looked like this:

820i	£18,446
820Si	£19,946
825Di	£20,946
820SLi	£21,946
825SDi	£22,446
Vitesse	£22,446
825Si	£22,446
825SLDi	£24,446
825SLi	£24,446
Turbo Coupé	£26,446
Sterling	£28,946
V6 Coupé	£30,446

Then, at the beginning of August, Rover announced two fleet orders for Sterlings, partly no doubt to help keep the cars in the public eye at a time when rumours were beginning to circulate about an eventual replacement. One of those fleet orders was fairly run-of-the-mill, for cars that would form the chauffeur-driven fleet to convey VIP passengers between Terminals 1 and 4 at London's Heathrow Airport. The other, however, was altogether more interesting, and created some unusual versions of the 800.

This second order was for an unspecified number of Sterlings to be used by the Bank of England's executive chauffeur fleet in the City of London. The Bank specifically requested dark leather upholstery, which was not available from the

In August 1996, a fleet of 800s was allocated to British Airways for courtesy car duties in connection with Concorde flights.

825Di	£19,200
820Si	£20,700
825SDi	£20,700
825i	£21,700
2.0 Sterling	£22,700
2.0 Sterling Coupé	£22,700
825Si	£23,200
Vitesse	£23,250
Vitesse Coupé	£23,250
2.5 Sterling	£26,250
2.5 Sterling Coupé	£26,250

The original plan had been for production of the Rover 800 range to come to an end in 1999, and to announce the replacement Rover 75 model at the Geneva Motor Show that March. However, Rover's owners at BMW discovered that the new Jaguar S-type – a competitor for their own 5 Series – was to be launched at the British International Motor Show in October 1998. As a result, they prevailed upon Rover to have their new car ready for launch at the same show, in order to steal some of the Jaguar's thunder. Rover complied, although there were then major delivery delays for the new 75 because the production lines had not begun assembling the new model in quantity. As they were put into the Cowley works, so assembly of the 800s wound down, and their production ceased without fanfare; the event was simply not newsworthy in the climate of the times.

Some 800s lingered on in the showrooms for a long time. At least two examples, one in British Racing Green and the other in Zircon Silver, are known to have acquired W-prefix registrations, which were not issued until March 2000 – some eighteen months after production had ended. The actual last-of-line car was built in Week 38 of 1998 (21–25 September) and was a White Gold 825 Sterling with the registration number T750 JVP. Its VIN was SARRSCLLKXM-260898. It was handed over to the Heritage Motor Centre collection but was subsequently sold off when the collection was slimmed down in July 2003. At the time of writing, it had disappeared.

Getting cars into the public eye remained important to Rover during the run-out period of the 800 range, as this was also the run-up period to the introduction of the Rover 75 in 1998. This one was used to transport South African president Nelson Mandela at the Commonwealth Conference in Edinburgh in October 1997.

PAINT AND TRIM OPTIONS – 1996–1998

1996 model year

There were seventeen paint options, of which four were solid types, seven were clearcoat metallics and six were pearlescents. In addition, on saloons and Fastbacks only, four of the pearlescent colours could be had with a complementary colour below the bump-strip level and a matching coachline; these were known as Duo Tone finishes. Black was available only to special order at extra cost. Coupés always came with blacked-out sills and lower bumpers, and with black bump-strips.

Most paints came with Stone Beige upholstery with contrasting piping, and there was a grey (Granite) alternative. Vitesse models always had Silverstone and Ash Grey half-leather upholstery unless supplied with the optional 'full leather' seat facings.

PAINT AND TRIM OPTIONS FOR 1996–1998

Paint	Default trim and carpet	Alternative trim and carpet
Black	Stone Beige with Prussian Blue	Granite with Ash
Bolero Red pearlescent	Stone Beige with Burgundy Red	Granite with Ash
Bolero Red with Pewter (Duo Tone)	Stone Beige with Burgundy Red	Granite with Ash
British Racing Green metallic	Stone Beige with Classic Green	Granite with Ash
British Racing Green pearlescent	Stone Beige with Classic Green	Granite with Ash
British Racing Green pearlescent with Willow (Duo Tone)	Stone Beige with Classic Green	Granite with Ash
Caspian Blue pearlescent	Stone Beige with Prussian Blue	Granite with Ash
Caspian Blue with Aegean (Duo Tone)	Stone Beige with Prussian Blue	Granite with Ash
Cayman Blue metallic	Stone Beige with Prussian Blue	Granite with Ash
Charcoal metallic	Stone Beige with Classic Green	Granite with Ash
Flame Red	Granite with Ash Grey	(none)
Midnight Blue	Stone Beige with Prussian Blue	Granite with Ash
Nightfire pearlescent	Stone Beige with Burgundy Red	Granite with Ash
Oxford Blue pearlescent	Stone Beige with Prussian Blue	Granite with Ash
Oxford Blue with Ionian (Duo Tone)	Stone Beige with Prussian Blue	Granite with Ash
Pewter Grey metallic	Stone Beige with Burgundy Red	Granite with Ash
White	Stone Beige with Classic Green	Granite with Ash
White Gold metallic	Stone Beige with Burgundy Red	Granite with Ash
Willow metallic	Stone Beige with Classic Green	Granite with Ash
Woodcote pearlescent	Stone Beige with Classic Green	Granite with Ash
Zircon Silver metallic	Stone Beige with Prussian Blue	Granite with Ash

1997 model year

The 1997 paint and trim options were the same as those for the 1996 model year except that Black was no longer listed. (It may nevertheless have been available to special order!) There was a change in April 1997, when Charleston Green metallic was added to the options list.

1998 model year

The 1998 paint and trim options were unchanged from those available at the end of the 1997 model year.

TECHNICAL SPECIFICATIONS – 1996–1998 MODELS

Engines
T-series 4-cylinder petrol
Iron block with aluminium alloy cylinder head
1994cc (84.5 x 89mm)
Twin ohc, belt-driven
4v per cylinder
Five-bearing crankshaft
Compression ratio 10.0:1
MEMS 1.9 multi-point injection
136PS (134bhp) at 6,000rpm
185Nm (136lb ft) at 2,500rpm with manual gearbox
176Nm (130lb ft) at 2,500rpm with automatic gearbox

T-series turbocharged 4-cylinder petrol
Iron block with aluminium alloy cylinder head
1994cc (84.5 x 89mm)
Twin ohc, belt-driven
4v per cylinder
Five-bearing crankshaft
Compression ratio 8.5:1
Garrett T25 turbocharger
MEMS multi-point injection
200PS (197bhp) at 6,100rpm
240Nm (177lb ft) at 2,000rpm

KV6 petrol
Aluminium alloy block and cylinder head
2497cc (80 x 83mm)
Two ohc on each cylinder bank, belt-driven
4v per cylinder
Four-bearing crankshaft
Compression ratio 10.5:1
MEMS 2J multi-point injection
175PS (173bhp) at 6,500rpm
240Nm (177lb ft) at 4,000rpm

VM HR 494 4-cylinder diesel (type 425 SLI RR)
Iron block with four individual aluminium alloy cylinder heads
2500cc (92 x 94mm)
Single ohc, gear-driven
2v per cylinder
Five-bearing crankshaft
Compression ratio 22.1:1

KKK turbocharger with intercooler and indirect injection
121PS (119bhp) at 4,200rpm
268Nm (197lb ft) at 1,900rpm

Transmission
Five-speed manual gearbox standard
   (4-cylinder petrol models; type PG1)
   Ratios 3.25:1, 1.89:1, 1.31:1, 1.03:1, 0.76:1; reverse 3.00:1
   (Diesel models; New Venture Gears type A568/T750)
   Ratios 3.31:1, 1.89:1, 1.27:1, 0.94:1, 0.71:1; reverse 3.00:1
   (KV6 models; type PG1)
   Ratios 3.17:1, 1.84:1, 1.31:1, 1.03:1, 0.76:1; reverse 3.00:1

Four-speed automatic gearbox optional:
   (4-cylinder models; ZF type 4HP 14)
   Ratios 2.41:1, 1.37:1, 1.00:1, 0.74:1; reverse 2.83:1
   (KV6 models; JATCO type JF403E)
   Ratios 2.78:1, 1.54:1, 1.00:1, 0.69:1; reverse 2.72:1

Axle ratio
3.47:1   KV6 models with automatic gearbox
3.50:1   Diesel models
3.94:1   KV6 models with manual gearbox
4.20:1   4-cylinder petrol and V6 models with manual gearbox
4.22:1   4-cylinder petrol models with automatic gearbox

Suspension, steering and brakes
Front suspension with unequal length double wishbones, steel coil springs and elastomeric compound spring aids, co-axial telescopic dampers and anti-roll bar
Rear suspension with independent struts, transverse and trailing links, steel coil springs and elastomeric compound spring aids, telescopic dampers and anti-roll bar
Uprated dampers and larger-diameter rear anti-roll bar on Vitesse
Rack-and-pinion steering with power assistance as standard: TRW Cam Gears type PCF on 4-cylinder models; Honda speed proportional type on V6 models
Disc brakes all round, with single-cylinder floating calipers; handbrake acting on rear discs
Ventilated front discs with 262mm diameter on 4-cylinder models and 285mm diameter on V6 models

TECHNICAL SPECIFICATIONS – 1996–1998 MODELS (continued)

Solid rear discs with 260mm diameter on all models

Two diagonally split hydraulic circuits; ABS standard on Vitesse and optional on all other models except 820

Dimensions

Overall length	192.2in (4,882mm)
Overall width	68.1in (1,730mm)
	76.9in (1,955mm) over mirrors
Overall height	54.8in (1,393mm)
Wheelbase	108.9in (2,766mm)
Front track	58.5in (1,486mm)
Rear track	57.1in (1,450mm)

Wheels and tyres

6J x 15 steel wheels with 195/65 VR 15 tyres on 820i, 820Si, 825D, 825SD and 825i

6J x 15 six-spoke alloy wheels with 195/65 VR 15 tyres on 820SLi, 825SLD and 825SLi

6J x 15 Prestige alloy wheels with 195/65 VR 15 tyres on Sterling

6J x 16 five-spoke Roversport alloy wheels with 205/55 VR 16 tyres on Vitesse

Kerb weight

Figures shown are for manual saloons; Fastbacks were 66lb (30kg) heavier across the range, and automatics another 33lb (15kg) heavier still.

2,944lb (1,335kg)	820i
2,977lb (1,350kg)	820Si
2,998lb (1,360kg)	820SLi
3,042lb (1,380kg)	825Si
3,075lb (1,395kg)	Vitesse
3,086lb (1,400kg)	825SLi
3,175lb (1,440kg)	825D
3,197lb (1,450kg)	825SD
3,219lb (1,460kg)	825SLD and Sterling

PERFORMANCE AND FUEL CONSUMPTION FIGURES, 1996–1998 MODELS

Acceleration and maximum speed figures are the ones claimed by the manufacturer. Fuel consumption is the composite average figure provided by the manufacturer.

	0-60mph	Maximum	Fuel consumption
820i, 820Si and 820SLi manual	10.0sec	125mph (201km/h)	35.3mpg (8ltr/100km)
820i, 820Si and 820SLi automatic	12.0sec	121mph (195km/h)	33.5mpg (8.4ltr/100km)
825Di, 825SDi and 825SLDi	10.7sec	124mph (199km/h)	46.1mpg (6.1ltr/100km)
Vitesse	7.3sec	143mph (230km/h)	34.9mpg (8.1ltr/100km)
827Si and 827SLi manual	8.2sec	135mph (217km/h)	33.4mpg (8.5ltr/100km)
827Si, 827SLi and Sterling automatic	9.5sec	131mph (211km/h)	32.5mpg (8.7ltr/100km)

CHAPTER EIGHT

AIMING HIGH: THE 800 COUPÉ

A coupé version of the 800 Series Rovers was planned from the very start of development in 1982 but it would be ten years before the car reached the showrooms. In that period, its fortunes waxed and waned. It was cancelled at least twice, and its key target market was wiped off the slate when Rover withdrew from the USA in 1991. But still it went into production.

The coupé derivative of the XX car formed part of the concept submission for the project examined by the Austin Rover Board during 1982. It was intended as a flagship product, and right from the start it was always intended to appeal primarily to the US market, where Rover expected to sell around 80–90 per cent of production. Americans were very keen on two-door coupés, and Rover's sights were set on the market that was being successfully exploited by the 3 Series BMW coupés and the Mercedes-Benz mid-range coupés (at that time, principally the 280CE).

PROJECT ANNA AND THE CCV

When Project XX got under way to design the Rover 800, work initially focused on the mainstream four-door saloons. However, design director Roy Axe was very keen on the coupé derivative, and in early 1984 he invited his designers to submit sketch proposals for such a car. It was normal practice to begin the design phase of a project with sketches, but this project 'was different to many others before it', remembers Steve Harper, who now runs his own design consultancy, Shado (www.shado.co.uk).

> [Axe] opened both the Exterior and the Interior design competition to all designers. This gave a long overdue chance for all of the designers to show their capability for both disciplines of design.

The coupé project was christened Project Anna within the design department, and the design eventually chosen for further development was one by Dave Saddington. It must have been a model based on this design that was shown to a dealer clinic in Chicago in the first half of 1985; as *Autocar* magazine reported in its issue dated 14 August 1985, US dealers estimated annual sales of more than 4,700 examples of the two-door car.

Meanwhile, Axe's designers had also been working on a concept car intended to revitalize the image of the MG marque, and that car (the MG EX-E) caused a sensation when it was displayed at the Frankfurt Motor Show in September 1985. Encouraged by the EX-E's reception, Axe realized that by creating a concept coupé based on the Rover 800 he could both promote the idea of the coupé more effectively within the company and drum up some excitement as a 'teaser' at motor shows in advance of the 800's launch. So during autumn 1985 he set his designers to work to create one.

The lead on creating the new Rover show model, known as the CCV (Coupé Concept Vehicle), was given to Gerry McGovern. McGovern had been responsible for the EX-E and

The Rover CCV was a 'glammed-up' concept that was based on work under way for the planned Coupé. This exterior sketch was produced by Gerry McGovern.

This was a design sketch for the interior of the CCV.

This sketch is thought to be one of those shown to US dealers in order to whet their appetites for the forthcoming Sterling Coupé. All the details of the production models appear to be in place, although the wheel design is fanciful.

was a natural choice for the job, although the basic design was actually Dave Saddington's work. The design was deliberately 'glammed-up', in Saddington's words, in order to have more of an impact. And an impact it certainly had when it was first seen in public at the Turin Motor Show in April 1986.

Autocar described it as a 'show stealer' in its issue of 23 April. *Motor* of 3 May complained that the car was hidden away at the back of the Austin Rover stand, but:

> this didn't stop a steady flow of the world's top designers seeking it out. The Rover has all the class and simple elegance that the Italians have forgotten about – to their cost. In the flesh the CCV has a serene presence, but above all it is hugely desirable. The Austin Rover design team were walking tall in Turin.

The CCV was actually closer than most people realize to the work that was going on to produce the new 800 Series coupé. However, the coupé now ran into the first of its many setbacks. As Harold Musgrove, Austin Rover's chairman and chief executive, explained to *Motor* magazine (issue of 28 June 1986), the coupé project had not yet gone in front of the Austin Rover Board. The coupé would find most of its buyers in the USA, and so Musgrove intended to wait and see how the Sterling saloons sold in North America. 'I don't see the CCV as a core car,' he said, 'and if it comes to a choice between CCV and a volume car, I will go for the volume model.'

Later that year, a review made clear that the cost of developing a coupé was too great for the resources available, and Project Anna was cancelled.

Nevertheless, two factors conspired to put the 800 coupé back on the Austin Rover agenda. The first was the enormously encouraging response from the USA to the launch of the Sterling derivatives of the 800 saloon. The second was the appearance in February 1987 of the Honda Legend Coupé. The Japanese company had been working independently on this car, without the knowledge of the British team; Honda also had very much the same market in mind as Rover had for their coupé. The result was that, even though Project Anna had been cancelled by Rover management, Roy Axe championed the coupé project whenever he got a chance. In due course he managed to get it reinstated among Rover's advance design programmes.

The question of cost was always paramount, and the product planning department insisted that an outside team should be asked to propose a coupé design, probably mainly to see whether more cost-effective design solutions were available. So the Italian design house of Bertone was contracted to produce an alternative (the Rover designers saw it as a rival) to the in-house design. When the two were compared, it was the in-house design that won out. As a next stage, Bertone were asked to turn the CCV design into a production car, but this project failed to meet the necessary financial targets and was taken no further.

Still undaunted, Roy Axe had the 'productionization' of Anna outsourced to IAD at Worthing, and Rover designer Chris Greville-Smith was assigned to oversee the transition from GRP concept to real metal car. The IAD car still clung quite closely to the ideas expressed in the CCV concept, but was a much more feasible production possibility. But once again, Anna failed to meet its cost targets.

THE ROVER CCV

The Rover CCV was unveiled on press day of the Turin Motor Show, 21 April 1986. The UK press release, embargoed until 20 April, described it as 'a design exercise exploring practical concepts … a logical extension of the philosophies that Austin Rover is applying to its future products. It is not intended for production'.

It was, however, built around the platform and running-gear of the forthcoming Rover 825, in left-hand-drive form to suit its intended market of the USA. Even though this was strictly a concept car, made largely of glass fibre, it was a drivable one – although that drivability was probably limited. The car was planned around electronically controlled dampers with a height-adjustment system front or rear that could raise the body to clear obstacles such as ferry ramps, although whether these actually worked on the concept car is unclear.

One way or another, the silver CCV was a dramatic style statement by the standards of 1986. Its lower body was recognizably related to that of the production 800 saloon, but the public could not have known that at Turin in April 1986. As befitted its US market orientation, the model was built with moulded impact-absorbing structures front and rear to meet US crash regulations. The upper body was particularly dramatic, looking as if it was made completely of glass. As on the MG EX-E, the roof panel was actually made of ceramic-coated polycarbonate over a steel frame, and incorporated a sunroof. There was flush glazing all round, with frameless door windows to give a pillarless look. Tests of the model had suggested that the drag coefficient would be a remarkably low 0.27.

Access to the cabin was by means of a card-key system, and the interior presented the CCV as a full four-seater. In the words of that UK press release, it blended:

prestigious elements with the luxury of a high quality sporting vehicle. This Rover house style coordinates the traditional British qualities of burr walnut and soft hide into a full wrap around theme of facia, doors and rear seat area.

ABOVE LEFT: **The CCV was designed to have a dramatic impact, and the full-size car certainly did. The low nose and narrow headlamps provided much of the drama in this view.**

ABOVE RIGHT: **The side view makes clear that the CCV was a fully practical proposition, even though it was designed as a show car.**

RIGHT: **From the rear, the CCV shows the dark glass and flush glazing that made the upper body look as if it was made completely from glass.**

Many of its features were very advanced for the mid-1980s, although it is quite hard to imagine their impact today, when so many have become commonplace on modern cars.

The CCV had a futuristic and somewhat cluttered liquid-crystal instrument display based around analogue-style dials. The minor switchgear was grouped in two small binnacles on either side of the steering wheel, and those binnacles also housed solid-state electronic displays relating to vehicle systems that included suspension settings, spoiler adjustment and the heating and ventilation system. The panel for the suspension settings was, admitted Roy Axe to *Motor* (issue of 26 April 1986), 'a bit of unashamed showmanship'. The centre console contained the ICE system, which featured a CD player and a hands-free cellular phone (again, as first seen in the EX-E). The console was also extended back between the individual rear seats, and included a video monitor, Video 8 cassette unit and remote controls for headphones.

The CCV would in fact be the last of the concept cars from Roy Axe's studio, because the company's product plan kept the design office fully occupied for the next few years. The car was later repainted a burgundy colour and now belongs to the collection of the British Motor Museum at Gaydon.

The CCV is seen here on a show stand during the set-up phase. The open door shows a fully practical interior with luxurious seats ...

... although the dashboard was a little too futuristic to be believable in 1986.

This was a full-size model of the real Coupé, which of course shared its lines with the 800 saloon introduced in 1986. Although the model has right-hand drive, it also incorporates the side markers that would be needed for the left-hand-drive US market.

into the sand. So the convertible went no further – but by this time Axe had been able to make a case for the coupé on cost grounds, and so Rover management finally agreed that it could be taken forward to production as part of the R17 programme to deliver a heavily facelifted 800 range.

The Project Anna coupé design was updated by Richard Woolley, and was then handed over to Dave Saddington to be turned into a production car. That Rover really did mean it this time was underlined by the US release in early 1990 of a concept sketch. This was a firm statement of intent – and then in 1991 the whole coupé project was once again thrown into turmoil when Rover decided to pull the Sterling marque out of the USA. With such a huge percentage of its planned sales now denied, the whole financial case for the coupé needed urgent review. On any rational grounds, the car should have been cancelled yet again, but by this stage the project was too far advanced for that. So it survived.

It was clear that the only way to get the coupé derivative approved for production was to reduce those costs, so Roy Axe now asked his designers to look at a car that shared much more with the 800 saloon. Whether earlier coupé designs had featured a shortened wheelbase (as in the Mercedes coupés) is not clear, but from now on there was no question that the Rover coupé would have to share the saloon's floorpan and therefore wheelbase.

Axe sought outside help yet again, this time adding spice to the project by looking at a convertible derivative of the coupé. Such a car had figured among the earliest design sketches in 1984, but this appears to be the first time that the idea was taken any further. The date would have been around 1989–90. Axe asked the American Sunroof Company (whose work was much more far-reaching than the company name suggested) to design a convertible version of Anna specifically for the US market. The liaison man at the Rover end was Adrian Griffiths, and the project delivered a most attractive car, which even had a removable hardtop of the kind available for the BMW convertibles. It also had a small Rover grille on the nose – and this, says Dave Saddington, was the start of the move back to using the grille to create a more clearly defined Rover 'face' across the range.

Sadly, this phase of the project also ran into problems. The convertible was put through a number of customer clinics in the USA and did not do well. Cost was against it, too, and by this time it was becoming clear that the attempt to sell the 800 with Sterling badges in the USA was also running

Work was also being done on a convertible version of the proposed coupé, and this design was produced for Rover by the American Sunroof Company. There would have been a detachable hardtop as an accessory.

This was another approach to the convertible project, in this case more obviously influenced by the shape of the CCV concept coupé.

Getting the proportions of the coupé right can not have been easy. Although the long wheelbase of the saloon ensured that there would be plenty of room for rear-seat passengers, it was the exterior design that needed special care. Dave Saddington and his team gave the coupé a more pronounced wedge shape than the saloon, and that ensured that every exterior panel would be unique to the two-door car. Even the front wings, superficially similar to those of the saloon, had a differently angled swage line; the boot lid, too, was different.

By the time the car was announced to the public at the 1992 Geneva Motor Show, it was known as the Rover 800 Coupé. There was only one version, with the 2.7-litre Honda V6 engine, so there was no need to call it an 827, as had been done with the saloon to distinguish the bigger-engined car from the smaller-engined 820 models. Why not Rover Sterling Coupé, as this was to be the flagship model and the Sterling was the top-of-the-range saloon? There seems to be no obvious reason.

One way or another, Rover had very high hopes for the new car. The Spring 1992 issue of *Catalyst* magazine (a Rover promotional tool given away in dealerships) called it 'a true

Later designs for the Coupé incorporated the more rounded lines planned for the R17 and R18 facelifted models. Note, though, that the model is labelled as an XX Coupé, using the project name of the first-generation 800s. Once again, US-market lighting was incorporated in this model, which was close to the final shape.

British coupé to challenge Audi, BMW and Mercedes both at home and in Europe'. Even so, those hopes were conservatively realistic. The car was to be built to order rather than for stock (an assertion that never again appeared in print), with deliveries commencing in June 1992.

The cost was always expected to be high, as befitted the new Rover flagship. The press release associated with the

An alternative design from late in the programme was this one, which used black-out roof supports to help re-create the effect of the CCV concept's top.

Designs included this stylish centre console between the rear seats, which was sadly not used on production models.

Somehow, the production Coupé had lost the drama suggested by the appetite-whetting sketch on p. 121, although there was no doubting that it was an attractive-looking car. Colour made quite a difference to its appearance, too, and in this case helps to show the black finish of the lower body sections. This early example would have been powered by the 2.7-litre Honda V6.

As this rear view shows, the Rover designers had very cleverly disguised the fact that the Coupé's wheelbase was no shorter than that of the saloon on which it was based.

Geneva Show claimed that the car was expected to cost about £32,000, at a time when a Sterling saloon cost just under £28,000. However, by the time it went on sale, the price had been fixed at a more realistic £30,770, or just over 10 per cent more than the top-model saloon. Only one extra-cost option was available, and that was a driver's side airbag, which cost £725. The 800 Coupé thus became the first British-built car sold in Europe with the option of such a device.

The car was certainly well equipped. Standard equipment with the 169PS (167bhp) engine was a four-speed automatic gearbox, but a five-speed manual could be had as a no-cost option. Power-assisted steering, ABS and cruise control were all standard. The paint options were all either metallic or pearlescent types, although solid Black was also listed. The wheels were 16in alloys, and there were twin bright tailpipes poking out from under the right-hand side of the rear bumper.

Inside, leather upholstery with a hand-stitched narrow-pleat design was standard (there was no alternative); it came in Light Stone Beige or Light Granite to suit the exterior colour, and had contrasting dark piping. There was leather on the steering wheel, the front grab handles, the head restraints, the door and rear body side trims, the cassette box lid between the seats, and the handbrake grip.

The front seats had electric adjustment with a position memory, which also covered the settings for the electrically operated door mirrors. Air conditioning, electric windows, an electric sunroof and central locking were all part of the specification; 'lazy locking', which automatically closed the sunroof and any open windows when the doors were locked, was also standard. The alarm system had both volumetric and perimetric sensing, and the ICE system was Rover's top-spec R990 stereo unit, with radio, cassette and CD functions, plus a six-CD changer located in the boot.

Although the dashboard was familiar fare, the plush-looking front seats were designed to tip forwards to give access to the rear. The seat release handle is clearly visible at the side of the top section in this picture.

THE 800 COUPÉ AND THE PRESS

The Rover press fleet had a demonstrator ready by the summer of 1992, and J710 SAC was finished in eye-catching Flame Red with a Stone Beige leather interior. It certainly looked the part, but from the moment that *Autocar & Motor* published their road-test impressions in the issue of 29 July 1992 it was clear that the car had missed its mark. 'This car aims to lift Rover a rung above the Fords, Vauxhalls and Peugeots that have historically provided the competition,' the report began, 'and to take a serious slant at an altogether different class of manufacturer, one epitomized by Mercedes and Jaguar.' The 'but' was almost palpable. The problem was that the car fell short in both performance and handling.

The engine lacked the power of those in obvious competitors from Jaguar (the XJ-S), Mercedes-Benz (the 300CE) and Audi (the S2). And although 'no other rival … can offer such civility from its engine … until the engine is controlled by a better-bred gearbox, [it] will continue to be compromised'. The four-speed EAT gearbox was criticized for harsh changes at low speeds and for slow responses in general.

The handling was simply lacklustre:

UK PRICES THROUGH THE YEARS			
1992, June	800 Coupé	£30,770	Launch price
1993, May	800 Coupé	£29,995	
1994, June	800 Coupé	£28,495	Response to Budget changes
1996, June	800 Turbo Coupé	£26,586	On-the-road price
	800 Coupé (KV6)	£30,586	On-the-road price
1996, December	2.0 Sterling Coupé	£22,340	
	Vitesse Coupé	£22,840	
	2.5 Sterling Coupé	£25,840	
1997, April	2.0 Sterling Coupé	£22,640	All 800 range prices increased
	Vitesse Coupé	£23,140	
	2.5 Sterling Coupé	£26,140	
1997, October	2.0 Sterling Coupé	£22,700	
	Vitesse Coupé	£23,250	
	2.5 Sterling Coupé	£26,250	

the hard truth Rover must face is that, compared with the standards set by those it must compete against, the 800 seems almost lame. … In reality, there is so little reward from pushing the Rover hard that you rarely bother to come close to the adhesion limits. … in almost any assessment of road ability, the Rover falls often far behind the standards of its rivals.

Even the car's styling:

split office opinion like no other in memory. The full range of comments from 'ungainly' and plain 'ugly' to 'pretty' and 'the best-looking car Rover has ever sold' were expressed.

The only really positive comment to come from the whole review was that 'for the first time in recent history, Rover has built a cabin with every bit as much class as you find in a Jaguar.' It was not enough – and the 800 Coupé has continued to divide opinions among commentators and enthusiasts ever since.

SALES AND NEW DERIVATIVES

The buying public seemed to agree, and the new 800 Coupé did not sell well. Although the exact figures are not available, a press release dated December 1996 – four-and-a-half

The Coupé was always a low-volume model, and very little changed over the years. This 1994 car shows no differences from the 1992 models.

years after the car had been launched – referred to sales of 'over 4,000' examples 'across Europe'. There were not many other countries where the car was actually sold (Japan

---

800 COUPÉ ACCESSORIES

There was a wide range of accessories available for the 800 Coupé, some of them of course shared with the 800 saloons. Many items were branded with the silver-on-maroon Rover logo. The list below relates to the 1994 and 1995 model years; some items were standard equipment in some overseas markets.

Booster cushion
Boot liner and mat
Bulb kit
Carry cot
Child seat
Cool box/oven
Cycle carrier
Dip converter
Driver's seat cover
Fire extinguisher
First aid kit
Floor mats (fabric)
Floor mats (rubber)
Headlamp covers
Headlamp power wash
Load carrier
Locking wheel nuts
Locking wheel nuts (alloy) – 1995 only

Luggage nets
Ratchet lashing straps
Roadside lamp – 1995 only
Roof bars
Security box (and installation kit)
Ski clips
Third brake light (mounted at base of rear window, inside glass)
Touch-up paints
Towbar, detachable
Towbar, fixed
Towing electrics (auxiliary)
Towing electrics (single)
Towing mirror
Tow stabilizer
Transmission oil cooler
Warning triangle
Zero temperature display (for ice warning) – 1995 only

---

was one), so that figure may translate to about 4,500 world-wide, or 1,000 Coupés a year. It was indeed a small-volume flagship.

One issue was that the Coupé was simply not special enough. It looked too much like the parent saloon, and it lacked the prestige of the German coupés against which it was competing; after being dragged through the mud in the British Leyland era, the Rover name no longer had its former cachet. Price was another issue. In May 1993 the 800 Coupé's price dropped to £29,995, at the same time as a driver's side airbag became standard. In December that year, prices rose across the Rover range by an average of 2.9 per cent – but the 800 Coupé's price remained unchanged. The June 1994 price drop to £28,495 reflected similar changes across the 800 range to make the cars more attractive after that year's Budget changed company car taxation. But the price crept back up again in June 1996. At that point, the Coupé became a two-model range, and the V6-engined car shot up to £30,586 as it gained the new KV6 engine and was joined by a cheaper (£26,586) 4-cylinder turbocharged derivative.

There were relatively few other changes in this first period of the Coupé's production. From April 1994, the cars gained a passenger's side airbag as standard, a rolling-code immobilizer linked to the central locking, a remote release for the boot lid and fuel filler on the centre console (in place of two separate levers on the floor), and an ana-logue clock. The second airbag was also made standard on Vitesse Sport and Sterling derivatives of the saloon, but was a £350 option on other models; it did not improve the appearance of the Coupé's dash, as the leather covering was somewhat crudely applied. The immobilizer, remote release and new clock were also standardized right across the 800 range.

THE KV6 CARS

When the KV6 engine was introduced in January 1996, it replaced the Honda V6 in all 800 Series models. As Chapter 7 explains, the former 827 models were now renamed 825 types. The Coupé retained its 800 Coupé name but benefited from a number of cosmetic changes when the new engine arrived. Many of these were shared with other 800 Series cars.

Most obvious was that KV6-engined Coupés had silver grille vanes instead of black items, bump-strips and bumper top cappings in the body colour, smoked lenses in the rear lights, and a new design of alloy wheel known as the Prestige style. The third brake light that had been optional was now standard equipment for all markets, and there were some new paint colours.

There were some changes inside, too. Upholstery was still available in only two colours, but the seat piping and

A change of wheels made a great difference to the Coupé's appearance. This is a very late example (the S-prefix registration shows that it was not put on the road until August 1998 or later) wearing the six-spoke alloy wheels that first became available on the 1996 models.

This is another late example, in this case with the Sterling specification and displaying the appropriate badge on its boot lid.

carpets were now in matching colours. So with Light Granite, the piping and carpets were in Ash Grey, but with Light Stone Beige the piping and carpets came in Burgundy Red, Classic Green or Prussian Blue to suit the exterior paintwork. All Coupés also had deep-pile overmats that matched the carpets and seat piping. On the door trims, the name

Rover was picked out in gold on the wooden fillets. There was a new ICE system, too; this time it was a Philips RD960 with RDS and CD changer.

Despite these changes, the Coupé was now beginning to feel a little old – or so thought Steve Cropley, writing of a KV6-powered example in *Autocar* dated 21 February 1996:

The later V6 models had the Rover KV6 engine in place of the Honda V6. This one was in a Japanese-market car.

The engine's fine. Strong, smooth, capable with an auto and evidently promising with a slick manual 'box. But the rest of the car is a snapshot of 1982. Reminds me irresistibly of an E-plate Rover 820 I had in 1991, except that the £2,000 nail rode better on smaller section tyres.

But while being rude about their car, I must confess some sympathy for the blokes that built it. Inside Rover, they know a good car as well as anyone, and it can only be reasons of budget, workload or politics that causes them to make one like this. Not preference.

THE TURBO COUPÉ

Since 1994, the fastest variant of the 800 range had not been the Honda V6-engined car but a new model called the Vitesse Sport.

A small number of 800s were painted in Charleston Green, a colour introduced in April 1997 for the 600-series Rovers but never listed in sales material. This Coupé was among them.

BELOW: **The turbocharged 4-cylinder Coupés carried a Vitesse badge on the boot lid, as here.**

This had a turbocharged derivative of Rover's 2-litre 4-cylinder T16 engine, and developed 200PS (197bhp). As the Coupé was supposed to be the Rover flagship, it was perhaps inevitable that this engine should eventually find its way into the two-door car to ensure that this was both the best-equipped and the fastest model in the range.

It took some time for this to happen, though. The new Turbo Coupé was not introduced until March 1996, and in fact lasted with that name only until December that year, when it was renamed a Vitesse Coupé. (In some overseas markets, it was always called an 820ti Coupé.) What caused the delay in the model's introduction is still unclear. It could have been that Rover's marketing people believed the Coupé was too much of a luxury-biased car to need the extra performance; or it could have been that only limited quantities of the turbocharged engines were being built and that the Coupé was not seen as one of the top priorities to receive it.

Nevertheless, the introduction of a second Coupé model alongside the new KV6-engined car did two things. First, it ensured that the flagship model would once again have the most powerful engine in the 800 Series range. Second, it allowed Rover to lower the entry-level price for the Coupé by a couple of thousand pounds. The new Turbo Coupé reached the showrooms at £26,586, while the price of the V6 car went up again, as already noted. Though the new turbocharged car was faster than the original 800 Coupé, its lower price could be justified by the smaller number of cylinders, the smaller engine capacity, and the slightly less refined nature of the turbocharged engine.

Sadly, the turbocharged engine added to the car's desirability but seems to have done little for sales. By this stage, the Coupé was beginning to look rather old-fashioned, and that made it hard to sell in the prestige-car market where up-to-the-minute styling was a vital factor.

Nevertheless, the Turbo Coupé was quite a car. It came only with a five-speed manual gearbox, and featured a torsen differential and the stiffer, 20mm lower, sports suspension used on the Vitesse Sport. The wheels were the same 17in six-spoke alloys as used on the Vitesse Sport, with 215/45 ZR 17 tyres. As for performance, a Turbo Coupé could reach 143mph (230km/h) and could accelerate to 60mph from standstill in 7.3sec; the 0–100km/h time was 7.8sec. All that plus a composite fuel economy of 34.9mpg (8.1ltr/100km) – at least, according to Rover – made it really rather special. Latterly with the Vitesse name, it remained in production until the end and, not surprisingly, it is still a much sought-after variant of the 800 Coupé.

THE FINAL THREE-MODEL RANGE

What happened next gives a fairly clear indication of how desperate Rover really were to inject some life into Coupé sales. In December 1996, the two-model Coupé range was expanded to three models, and the two existing models were renamed.

The third Coupé model expanded the range downwards,

A SPECIAL SHOW COUPÉ

BMW was keen to make a big impression at the 1997 Frankfurt Motor Show, not only with its own products but also with the products of its British affiliate. To that end, the British brands were all encouraged to produce something special. Mini showed some extreme concepts; MG showed the EX-F land speed record car and a special-edition MGF; Land Rover launched its new Freelander and created a special long-wheelbase motorbike tender (which was designed to carry the new BMW 1200C cruiser motorbike); and Rover came up with the 200 BRM and 425 V6 concepts, and a special 800 Coupé.

The special Coupé was designed largely by Martin Peach, who was responsible for colour and trim in the Rover design studio and was also in charge of special editions. He told David Morgan some years ago that he had been asked by Tom Purves, Rover Group's new sales and marketing director, to look at various schemes for a one-off show car. His design was executed by a bespoke retrim business on behalf of the design studio, and was shown at Frankfurt in September 1997 as the Coachbuilt 800 Coupé. Martin later admitted that he felt the design was not an entirely happy mix of history and modernity.

The car was a left-hand-drive example, finished in Bolero Red and wearing six-spoke alloy wheels. The interior was upholstered in beige and burgundy twin-stitched leather, with a two-tone facia and carpets in Wildberry with a beige binding. There was burr walnut on the centre console, facia, door inserts and picnic tables on the backs of the front seats. These picnic tables featured chrome glass-retainer inserts. Seat lifters, door clocks and controls were all chrome plated, and a chessboard was incorporated within the centre rear armrest, illuminated by a light from within the armrest aperture.

'The Rover 800 Coupé concept is an exposition of the character of Rover,' read the press release, 'and will not be available for sale.' The car was shown at Frankfurt with a similarly coloured Rover 3-litre Coupé from the first half of the 1960s, one of the models that had inspired the concept Coupé's design.

A special 'coachbuilt' Coupé was prepared for the 1997 Frankfurt Motor Show. This publicity photo shows that it was intended to evoke the classic Rovers of earlier times, such as the P5 3-litre Coupé in the background. The special interior was extremely attractive, but it came too late in the Coupé's lifetime to have any chance of becoming a regular production option.

weighing-in at £3,500 less than the KV6 model and £500 less than the turbocharged car. Once again, it seems to have made precious little difference to sales but was rather a classic case of 'too little, too late'. Yet for all that, the new 2.0 Sterling Coupé was an interesting car. With its arrival, the existing two models became the Vitesse Coupé and the 2.5 Sterling Coupé, although the badges on the cars did not change.

The engine was the 2.0-litre type from the Rover 820 saloon, with 136PS (134bhp) and 185Nm (136lb ft) of torque. With the five-speed manual gearbox that was standard, the car would reach 60mph from rest in 10sec and go on to 125mph (201km/h); with the extra-cost automatic gearbox, its top speed was 121mph (195km/h) and the 0–60mph time went up to around 12sec. The 2-litre Coupé came with all the features of its more powerful brothers except for cruise control, which was simply not available at all.

How many of these cars were built remains an open question. As we have seen, Coupé production up to the end of 1996 was around 1,000 cars a year; it probably slowed down after that. If the 2-litre model took one-third of sales in the eighteen months of its production from January 1997 to mid-1998, there would have been 500 cars. In practice, the car probably sold more slowly than its two more powerful siblings, so it would be reasonable to suppose that there were fewer than 500 built. This makes a 2.0 Sterling Coupé at least rare, if not necessarily precious and beautiful as well.

LOOKING BACK

So was the 800 Coupé a success? In most respects, it was not. From its manufacturer's point of view, it sold too slowly ever to justify the amount of effort that had gone into its creation. It was an attractive but somehow almost invisible car, not being sufficiently distinctive to attract the clientele at whom it was aimed. From the point of view of an owner, it was a well-finished, well-equipped and reasonably reliable car that was capable of a fair turn of speed, especially in turbocharged form.

Today, the 800 Coupé has rarity on its side, but at a time when its siblings have fallen firmly into the cheap banger category, it appeals only to those who really understand what it is. For the future, then, it seems likely that a good proportion of surviving cars will succumb to the ill treatment and neglect that usually accompany impecunious ownership of an expensive car. The result will surely be that the 800

Coupé becomes an even rarer species and, if it does become more widely appreciated, good examples will then probably command quite high prices.

800 COUPÉ PRODUCTION FIGURES

No reliable production figures for the 800 Coupé were known at the time of writing although, as noted in the main text, production of around 1,000 cars a year can be estimated from figures released by Rover Group. As the cars were in production for six-and-a-half years, from March 1992 until September 1998, there would therefore have been around 6,500 in all. Allowing for slightly higher production during the 'honeymoon period' of the first year or so, the figure might have reached 7,000.

This matches quite well figures posted on the Rover 800 internet forum by somebody who was involved in despatching body panels from the pressing plant at Swindon to the assembly lines at Cowley. He claims that around 90 sets of panels were shipped each month and that the 79 months between March 1992 and October 1998 would give a total of 7,110 cars. (Note that some sources claim production ended in October 1998, but that would have been a month after the official last-of-line Rover 800 was built.)

Some variants were clearly less numerous than others. The 820 Vitesse Coupé, for example, was in production for only 20 months (January 1997 to September 1998), while the 820 Coupé was built for only 31 or 32 months (January 1996 to September or October 1998). It is thought that most of the 820 Coupés were left-hand-drive models destined for Italy, where tax laws favoured their 2-litre engines.

Rover submitted annual build figures to the SMMT, but only partial figures are available. Those for 820 and 825 models in 1996–1997 are not accompanied by those for Vitesse variants, but looked like this:

	1996	1997	1998
820	9	574	399
825	269	382	384
Total	**278**	**956**	**783**

COLOURS AND TRIMS

Between 1992 and 1995, the Coupé models were available with a limited selection of colours from the 800 Series palette. For the 1996–1998 model years, they were available with all the 800 Series colour options except for the two-tones.

1992–1995 model years

There were seven paint colours and two interior colour options. Upholstery was always in leather.

Paint type	Colour	Interior Standard	Interior Optional
Metallic	Black	Light Stone Beige	Light Granite
	British Racing Green	Light Stone Beige	Light Granite
	Quicksilver	Light Granite	Light Stone Beige
	Storm Grey	Light Granite	Light Stone Beige
	White Gold	Light Stone Beige	Light Granite
Pearlescent	Caribbean Blue	Light Stone Beige	Light Granite
	Nightfire Red	Light Stone Beige	Light Granite

1996–1998 model years

There were sixteen paint colours and two interior colour options. There were two versions of British Racing Green, one a metallic and the other a pearlescent paint. Upholstery was always in leather. Granite leather (with Ash Grey carpets) was available with all colours; Stone Beige leather came with piping and carpets to suit the body colour, as listed below.

Paint type	Colour	Carpet colour with Stone Beige
Solid	Flame Red	(Not available with Stone Beige)
	Midnight Blue	Prussian Blue
	White	Green
Metallic	British Racing Green	Classic Green
	Caspian Blue	Prussian Blue
	Charcoal	Classic Green
	Pewter Grey	Burgundy
	White Gold	Burgundy
	Willow	Classic Green
	Zircon Silver	Prussian Blue
Pearlescent	Bolero Red	Burgundy
	British Racing Green	Classic Green
	Caspian Blue	Prussian Blue
	Nightfire Red	Burgundy
	Oxford Blue	Prussian Blue
	Woodcote	Classic Green

From approximately April 1997, small numbers of cars were painted in Charleston Green.

CHAPTER NINE

800 SPECIALS

There were several special derivatives of the Rover 800 during its production life. Some were aftermarket developments, such as the Janspeed turbocharged car; some were factory-developed 'specials', such as the police-specification models; and others were factory-approved conversions, such as the armoured derivatives and the long-wheelbase limousines and hearses.

ARMOURED ROVER 800s

It is no surprise that very little hard information is available about armoured versions of the Rover 800: the precise details of such armouring are not disclosed in order to make it harder for would-be attackers to determine where the weak spots might be. Nevertheless, it is clear that an armoured 800 was available by 1987, so the probability is that its development had begun before the 800 was actually released to the public.

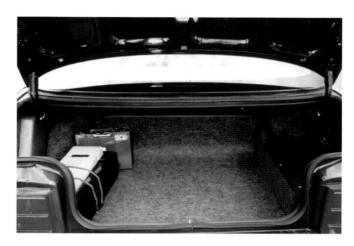

A view inside the boot reveals some differences from the standard car. Behind the rear seat (here concealed by the carpet) was an oxygen supply system designed to help the car's occupants survive a poison gas attack. TANK MUSEUM, BOVINGTON, VIA GEOFF FLETCHER

The British armed forces bought this armoured 800-series saloon sometime around 1987. It was based on an 825i model and was probably armoured by MacNeillie's of Walsall. There is very little to give the game away in these pictures of the exterior, although a close look reveals differences around the window frames, thicker than standard blackout lines around the windscreen and rear window, and a black metal panel instead of the rearmost side window. TANK MUSEUM, BOVINGTON, VIA GEOFF FLETCHER

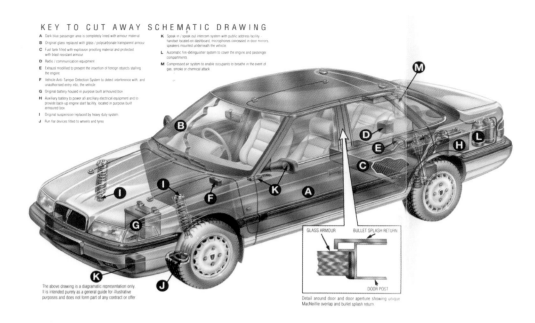

KEY TO CUT AWAY SCHEMATIC DRAWING

A Dark blue passenger area is completely lined with armour material
B Original glass replaced with glass / polycarbonate transparent armour
C Fuel tank fitted with explosion proofing material and protected with blast resistant armour
D Radio / communication equipment
E Exhaust modified to prevent the insertion of foreign objects stalling the engine
F Vehicle Anti-Tamper Detection System to detect interference with, and unauthorised entry into, the vehicle
G Original battery housed in purpose built armoured box
H Auxiliary battery to power all ancillary electrical equipment and to provide back-up engine start facility, located in purpose built armoured box
I Original suspension replaced by heavy duty system
J Run flat devices fitted to wheels and tyres

K Speak in / speak out intercom system with public address facility, handset located on dashboard, microphones concealed in door mirrors, speakers mounted underneath the vehicle
L Automatic fire-extinguisher system to cover the engine and passenger compartments
M Compressed air system to enable occupants to breathe in the event of gas, smoke or chemical attack

The above drawing is a diagramatic representation only. It is intended purely as a general guide for illustrative purposes and does not form part of any contract or offer.

GLASS ARMOUR   BULLET SPLASH RETURN

DOOR POST

Detail around door and door aperture showing unique MacNeillie overlap and bullet splash return.

This drawing from a MacNeillie sales brochure shows the features of a post-1991 armoured Rover 800. Not every car would have the same features, of course: they would be chosen to meet the perceived threat.

This explains those differences around the window frames: the door windows, though electrically powered as in the standard car, were made of thick armoured glass. TANK MUSEUM, BOVINGTON, VIA GEOFF FLETCHER

The evidence suggests that Rover worked closely with S. MacNeillie & Son Ltd of Walsall, who specialized in stretched limousine and armour-plating work, to develop the car. Certainly, it was MacNeillie's who offered a factory-approved armoured derivative of the facelifted cars after 1992. At least one car, based on an 825Si, was delivered to the Ministry of Defence testing grounds at Chertsey in Surrey, and its serial number indicates a 1987 contract. Its exact use is of course not clear, although it was a left-hand-drive car and

was therefore not intended for use in mainland Britain or in Northern Ireland.

THE LONG-WHEELBASE 800s

Rover were well aware of a limited market for extended-wheelbase cars such as limousines and hearses, but that market was too small for them to consider offering such derivatives themselves. There had been no extended-wheelbase versions of earlier big Rovers, but the front-wheel-drive configuration of the 800 Series made the car attractive as the basis for such models: when extending the wheelbase, there was no need for the additional complication of an extended drive-line to the rear wheels.

It looks as if Rover started looking around for a company or companies to build such derivatives as a semi-private venture (but with 'factory approval') soon after the 800 entered production. As things were to turn out, it entered into agreements with two separate specialists, Startins of Birmingham and Coleman Milne of Bolton. The vehicle types were divided carefully between them, Startins developing a long-wheelbase model for the funeral trade and Coleman Milne developing a rather different long-wheelbase model for the chauffeur-drive market. Both reached the market before the end of the decade, the Startins model slightly before the Coleman Milne car.

Startins developed a companion-model hearse to suit their customers. It is not clear when this became available, but it was probably at the same time as the limousine, in 1988. Both Startins and Coleman Milne then adapted their original designs to suit the facelifted Rovers introduced in October 1991. However, in 1992 Rover Group decided to reallocate the contract for its chauffeur-driven 800 derivatives from Coleman Milne to Startins, with the result that Startins would be responsible for all the extended-wheelbase 800s. In practice, the changeover did not occur until mid-1994.

A further complication occurred in February 1995, when the Startins coachbuilding business was bought by S. MacNeillie & Son Ltd of Walsall, who specialized in stretched limousine and armour-plating work. Production of all the Startins Rover 800 derivatives was transferred to Walsall, and they were thereafter marketed under the MacNeillie name. The last examples were probably built in early 1999, using some of the final production 800 models built the previous autumn.

The Startins Models

Thomas Startin Jnr Ltd of Birmingham was both an Austin Rover dealership and a small-volume coachbuilder working primarily on commercial vehicles. Nevertheless, by the 1980s Startins had secured a good position in the market for funeral vehicles, building both long-wheelbase limousines and hearses. In search of an alternative to the ubiquitous Ford Granada base vehicle, the company turned to the Rover 800.

Startins probably began work on their Rover 800 conversions during 1987, aiming to create both types on the same wheelbase, which added 33in (838mm) to the standard dimension to make a wheelbase of 141.6in (3,597mm). Close cooperation with the Rover Group enabled Startins to put their prototype through an extensive test programme at Rover's Gaydon proving ground. It looks as if the limousine version became available during 1988, and the hearse probably became available at the same time. The first production models all had the 2.7-litre V6 engine, although it is possible that prototypes may have been converted from earlier 2.5-litre cars.

The limousines were marketed under the name of the Startins Regency. They retained a four-door configuration, the extra length being inserted behind the rear doors where

Startins focused their efforts on creating 800 derivatives for the funeral trade. Seen here are early examples of their six-door limousine and the companion hearse. They were photographed on delivery to the Co-Operative Funeral Service at Ilkeston in Derbyshire.

The overall lines of the hearse are clear in this photograph of a 1991 model, which appears to have been fitted with the grille made available by Austin Rover to update the appearance of the early R8 200 Series cars.

an additional side window accompanied the extended rear 'wing' panel. There was a glass division between the driving and rear passenger compartments, and two rearward-facing folding 'jump seats' in the centre made the seating capacity up to seven. However, some sources quote a seating capacity of eight, which implies that the driving compartment had a bench seat for three people.

Startins were able to get some good publicity for their new model when they sold an early example to the National Exhibition Centre (NEC) at Birmingham, where it was used for transporting VIP visitors. The car also sold steadily but in small numbers to the funeral trade, for which it had been primarily designed. Some businesses took matching fleets of Startins Regency limousines and Startins 800 hearses, and among them was the Co-operative Society, which was then the leading chain of undertakers in the UK.

Startins adapted their designs to the facelfted Rovers introduced in 1991, and the first examples of these new models were ready by late 1992. Meanwhile, the company had also been working on a six-door model, this time with a 36in (914mm) extension to give a total wheelbase of 144.6in (3,673mm). This reached the market during 1993, and was supposedly aimed less at the funeral trade and more at the VIP transport and hotel taxi business. It incorporated a for-ward-facing centre row of three seats, which made it capable of carrying eight people. The design of the window in the centre door was arguably a little awkward, but overall the six-door car worked quite well.

Startins thus had three separate models in production by the end of 1993: the four-door funeral limousine and the hearse, both on the 141.6in wheelbase, and the six-door 'hotel taxi' on the 144.6in wheelbase. They were soon to have a fourth model. As already explained, Rover decided in 1992 that Startins should take over production of the chauffeur-driven limousine from Coleman Milne. In practice, Coleman Milne did not build their last example until May 1994, and in July that year Startins announced a modified version of their four-door Regency design to replace it. This did not take on the Vanden Plas name from the earlier Coleman Milne design but was known as a Regency LSE. The letters stood for 'Long Saloon, Executive', but it can hardly be a coincidence that the same letters

The six-door Startins conversion remained available for the facelifted models. This one was based on an 827Si model and was new to the Co-Operative Funeral Service in Glasgow, being registered on 1 August 1996. By that stage, new V6 models had the Rover KV6 engine; based on the 'old' model, this car would have taken several months to convert. It was actually built by MacNeillie's at Walsall.

STARTINS LONG-WHEELBASE PRODUCTION FIGURES

Figures provided to David Morgan by Martin Clive, formerly specialist vehicle sales manager at MacNeillie's, show that there were just under 300 long-wheelbase cars using the Startins designs. Although the breakdown of individual types is incomplete, the overall picture seems clear.

	Regency	Regency LSE	Six-door	Hearse	Total
Startins, 1988–95	N/K	2	9 (approx.)	N/K	155
MacNeillie, 1995–99	N/K	11	N/K	N/K	141
				Total	**296**

Note that 61 of the MacNeillie conversions were based on cars with the Rover KV6 engine.

with it. MacNeillie's invested in new production facilities, and production of the Regency, Regency LSE, six-door limousine and hearse was transferred to Walsall. MacNeillie's also made some improvements to the folding occasional seats in the Regency models. An interesting sideline is that some cars were supposedly converted from saloons and others started life as Fastbacks; perhaps MacNeillie's simply took whatever was most readily available at the time. Production continued until 1999, by which time the company was ready with limousine and hearse derivatives of the Rover 75, which replaced the 800 range.

were already in use for the long-wheelbase Range Rover. On the Range Rover Vogue LSE, the letters were nevertheless said to stand for 'Long-wheelbase, Special Equipment'. The Regency LSE was priced at £35,000 plus on-the-road charges.

When MacNeillie's took over the Startins coachbuilding business in early 1995, all four Rover 800 derivatives went

The Coleman Milne Rover 800 Vanden Plas

Coleman Milne were a Bolton company well known by the 1980s for their long-wheelbase limousine conversions based on large saloon cars. Founded in 1953, initially as vehicle body builders and repairers, the company began in the late 1950s to focus on specialized coachbuilt limousines. During 1983

The Coleman Milne long-wheelbase limousine was introduced in 1989 and became known as the Rover Vanden Plas. It was normally based on an 827 Sterling, like this example.

The main purpose of the Coleman Milne 'stretch' was to create additional lounging room in the back.

they took over one of their main rivals, Woodall Nicholson of Halifax, and in late 1985 they became a wholly owned subsidiary of the Henly Group (through Henlys Holdings Ltd). By the end of the 1980s, Coleman Milne were building around 300 vehicles a year and employed 120 staff.

Among those vehicles was already a long-wheelbase version of the Austin Montego, and the request for a Rover 800 limousine followed quite naturally. For Coleman Milne, the timing was ideal as it was was looking for a new product to replace its conversion of the Daimler DS420 limousine, whose production was being wound down.

The aim of this limousine conversion was to provide maximum legroom in the rear rather than to make room for more passengers, so Coleman Milne went for a more modest 12in (305mm) wheelbase extension, making the full wheelbase 120.6in (3,063mm). The first car was built in early 1989 and was registered that May, almost certainly as F347 SWK. The company based its conversion on a Sterling in order to benefit from that model's high level of equipment.

Within Coleman Milne, the car was known as the Executive, and in fact that name was used for the first eleven examples built. However, in May 1989 Austin Rover gave permission for the model to be called the Rover 800 Vanden Plas, and Vanden Plas badges were added thereafter.

None of those first eleven cars was finished in black, and the example displayed at the London Motorfair in October 1989 on the Coleman Milne stand was in Cherry Red pearlescent with a red leather interior. Inside, the Motorfair car had a specially redesigned rear seat with extra width in the base and an over-cushion for extra comfort. However, this was an optional extra; normally, the limousine simply had the Sterling's electrically adjusted rear seat option, and its extra legroom allowed this to be used to the full. The longer rear door trims each incorporated an ashtray and a cigarette lighter, together with special burr walnut trim to match that in the rest of the car.

A rear floor console was standard, borrowed from the US-market Sterling, and an overhead lamp cluster and fluorescent lights built into the rear quarter panel provided light for working while on the move. The centre rear armrest was modified to create a box that could carry a mobile phone or other equipment, although it could still be folded back into the seat if required. The finishing touches were footrests and over-rugs for the rear compartment.

By the time of the 1989 Motorfair, Coleman Milne were claiming to have attracted orders for twenty cars. In practice, most of the first-generation Coleman Milne 800 limousines were built for Rover Cars in the UK or for Rover Japan. In October 1989, the price of the conversion began at £13,500 plus appropriate taxes, and complete cars could be had from around £40,000.

Cars were probably always built to order rather than for stock, and each one took between three and four months to complete. Part-finished Rover Sterlings were shipped from Cowley to Bolton, where they were mounted on a jig and carefully cut into two down the middle. The floorpan and roof were then extended by 12in (305mm), and the rear doors were lengthened to suit. At the same time, the passenger cabin's rear superstructure was modified to provide a longer rear quarter panel, which gave more privacy for the occupants of the rear seat. An option on these pre-1991 cars was a solid rear panel in place of the rear quarter glass, to give additional occupant privacy.

When the facelifted R17 version of the 800 entered production, Coleman Milne simply adapted their existing conversion to suit it, one change being that the solid rear panel ceased to be available. As explained above, Rover Group then decided to reallocate the contract for its chauffeur-driven 800 derivatives to Startins. As a result, the Coleman Milne version went out of production, and the last examples were built in May 1994.

David Morgan reports being told in January 2003 by Kevin Heath of Coleman Milne that a total of twenty-five limousines were built, although the exact division between XX and R17-based cars was not clear. Although some cars were black, there were also some in metallic green (possibly British Racing Green), some in white and some in red (including the 1989 Motorfair car).

JANSPEED TURBO

Janspeed Engineering had built up an excellent reputation for its work with turbocharging in the 1970s, and during the 1980s offered turbocharger conversions for Rover SD1 models and Range Rovers, among many others. During the second quarter of 1987, it announced the availability of a conversion for the Rover 820i.

Motor magazine tried out a converted 820Si model for its issue of 5 March 1988. The conversion was still under development at that stage, and Janspeed had imposed restraints in order to keep costs down. So the turbocharged engine developed an already impressive 183bhp at 5,500rpm and 186lb ft at 3,000rpm. For comparison, the standard engine put out 138bhp at 6,000rpm and 131lb ft at 4,500rpm.

Frank Swanston, Janspeed's development manager, said that the engine could be further developed to give 'well over 200bhp. It can handle it. We're impressed with the way Rover have built this [M16] engine. Frankly, it's not what we're used to from them.' As it was, the turbo boost was limited to a modest 7psi, and the engine was able to run with a 9.0:1 compression (achieved by machining the standard pistons), which was high for a turbocharged type. The basis of the conversion was a water-cooled Rotomaster R60 turbocharger with an aluminium air-to-air intercooler ahead of the radiator and a Rajay wastegate. To this were added a fabricated stainless-steel, pulse-tuned exhaust manifold, a low back-pressure exhaust system and a Zytek ECU appropriately mapped by Janspeed.

Motor wondered whether adding even more power and torque would be worth the trouble, because the current tune made such a huge improvement over the standard car. The 0–60mph sprint was despatched in 7.7sec, which made

The Janspeed turbocharged conversion of the multi-point injection M16 engine promised huge performance. This was the company's demonstrator, decked out with their own body kit and special wheels.

the Janspeed car quicker than the latest 800s with the 2.7-litre Honda V6 engine. Although the top speed was only 0.5mph better than the standard car, at 126.9mph (204km/h), Janspeed believed that 130mph (209km/h) or slightly more would be achievable with a remapped ECU.

'The standard engine seems gutless by comparison,' argued *Motor*.

> *Compounding the impression is the engine's power delivery; it does not feel or behave as if it is turbocharged but like a more muscular version of the original. ... The Rover engine ... rouses from its light slumber at around 2,500rpm and is spinning lustily by 4,000rpm. From behind the wheel, the sensation is no more dramatic than that of a powerful engine coming on cam.*

Although turbocharged engines of the era were notorious for poor bottom-end performance (below the speed at which the turbocharger became effective), this one had respectable low-down urge and gave effective engine braking on the overrun.

Janspeed had not done any development on the car's suspension, even though the company did advertise the availability of wheel, tyre and suspension modifications for the 800 range. *Motor* reported that:

*the only chassis flaw is one that affects all the big
Rovers: a tendency for the lightly loaded front wheel
to tramp under power in corners that induce a lot of
body roll.*

The cost of the conversion was £2,805 plus VAT, but Janspeed recommended an uprated clutch for a further £110. So a new 820Si with the Janspeed conversion worked out at £18,450 – more than the cost of a new 827SLi. The converted car's fuel consumption was also higher, and *Motor* quoted a figure of 22.5mpg (12.6ltr/100km) as against 23.3mpg (12.1ltr/100km).

The test car was also fitted with a Janspeed body kit, made for them by Auto Engineering and priced at nearly £1,400. It was, said *Motor*, 'superbly fitted but ostentatious and does the Rover no favours'.

It is not clear how many Rover 800s were converted by Janspeed, but there cannot have been many. Demand also seems not to have been high enough for the company to develop the promised 200bhp version.

ROVER 800s IN UK POLICE SERVICE

Rover had sold a good number of its SD1 models to police forces in the UK, and from the start had every intention of repeating this success with the 800 range. So at least two police demonstrators were prepared very early on and were

registered as C472 AKV and C474 AKV. Both were 825i models, but with the cheaper interior trim and equipment of the entry-level 820E. C474 AKV had the optional five-speed manual gearbox, and C472 AKV may have done, too.

Autocar magazine got to try C474 AKV in a fascinating back-to-back test of four demonstrator cars that were competing for police business as replacements for the SD1. The other three cars were a Jaguar XJ6 3.6, a Vauxhall Senator 3.0i and a Ford Sierra 4x4. The report was published in *Autocar's* issue of 25 March 1987. There were no real winners, although the test team favoured the Ford for its road-holding ability. As for the Rover, they noted that the rooftop light bar reduced maximum speed from the standard car's 131mph (211km/h) to just 118mph (190km/h). They added that, 'we liked the Rover as a patrol car because of its excellent all-round blend of performance, handling and real refinement.'

Despite resistance to front-wheel drive in some forces, police orders for the Rover followed quite swiftly. Early deliveries were of 825i models, but some forces took the 820i and there were several deliveries of 827i and later 827SLi types. Both saloon and Fastback derivatives entered police service.

Although no full list of UK police forces that bought first-generation Rover 800s is available, information from various sources, including the records of the Police Vehicle Enthusiasts' Club (www.pvec.org.uk), shows that examples were definitely taken on by the following twelve forces; there were undoubtedly more:

C472 AKV was an early police demonstrator, and is seen here in fairly typical 'jam sandwich' livery, almost certainly while on loan to the West Mercia Constabulary. The force would go on to buy several 800s for its contribution to the Central Motorway Group.

Seen in a typical location overlooking a busy motorway, this is **C472 AKV** during its time with the West Mercia Constabulary.

Again wearing 'jam sandwich' livery, this 827i belonged to the Central Scotland Police. The actual livery used on patrol cars of course varied from one force to the next, as did items of equipment like the roof-mounted light bar. POLICE VEHICLE ENTHUSIASTS' CLUB

Avon & Somerset Constabulary
Central Scotland Police
Cheshire Constabulary
Cumbrian Constabulary
Dyfed Powys Police
Dumfries & Galloway Police

Greater Manchester Police
Isle of Man Police
Metropolitan Police
Strathclyde Police
West Mercia Police
West Midlands Police

In addition, many examples were used by the Central Motorway Group, which combined officers and vehicles from the West Midlands, West Mercia and Staffordshire forces.

By the time of the 800's facelift in 1991, the model had become well established as a patrol car. Many forces had chosen not to standardize on any one SD1 replacement, but to run Rovers alongside Vauxhall Senators and Ford

143

Not every police 800 was V6-powered. This 1990-model 820i Fastback belonged to the Strathclyde Police. POLICE VEHICLE ENTHUSIASTS' CLUB

This early 825i was used by the **Cumbrian Constabulary,** who sent the photograph to Rover's fleet sales manager, David Millard. The car had covered 100,000 trouble-free miles and returned an average of 24.2mpg (11.7ltr/100km) by the time it was returned to Rover. An order for five 827 patrol cars followed in 1988. The notice on the bonnet reads, 'For Sale. 100,000 miles, one careful owner. (Never had wick turned up.) For details, contact David Millard.'

This 1989 Metropolitan Police 827 Fastback was pictured in preservation. The roof-mounted light bar and broad side stripe are different yet again. Note the inscription on the rear wing: 'Video Equipped'.

The Fastback models were also much liked by some police forces in the UK. This one belonged to the Cheshire Constabulary, who favoured a yellow side stripe and a single large blue light rather than a roof bar. POLICE VEHICLE ENTHUSIASTS' CLUB

Granadas. Both saloon and Fastback variants of the facelifted cars entered police service, most of them being 820i or 827i types. Nevertheless, Rover did prepare an 820 Turbo 16v Fastback as a police demonstrator, and K840 ADU eventually entered service with the Northumbria Police.

Once again, no full list of UK police forces that bought second-generation Rover 800s is available. The records of the Police Vehicle Enthusiasts' Club show that examples were definitely taken on by the following eighteen forces; there were undoubtedly others:

Central Scotland Police
Devon & Cornwall Police
Dorset Police
Durham Constabulary
Grampian Police
Humberside Police
Lancashire Police
Leicestershire Constabulary
Lothian & Borders Police

Metropolitan Police
Northern Constabulary
Northumbria Police
South Wales Police
South Yorkshire Police
Strathclyde Police
Surrey Police
Thames Valley Police
West Midlands Police

As with the first-generation cars, several second-generation 800s were used by the Central Motorway Group.

The Coventry registration number on this Central Scotland car suggests it may once have been a Rover demonstrator – or perhaps it was supplied on long-term loan as an incentive for the force to buy more. This example of a facelifted model was probably an 827i. POLICE VEHICLE ENTHUSIASTS' CLUB

Once again, the Coventry registration suggests an ex-demonstrator or a long-term loan car. This 1993 827i was pictured on the strength of the Devon and Cornwall Police. POLICE VEHICLE ENTHUSIASTS' CLUB

Yet another livery is in evidence on this 1995 827i that belonged to the Metropolitan Police, with reflective silver panels on the white background anticipating later police use of 'Battenburg' livery. The car was allocated to the Special Escort Group, and was photographed by the River Thames, near the Met's famous Barnes Traffic Garage. POLICE VEHICLE ENTHUSIASTS' CLUB

The police were not the only emergency service to buy examples of the 800. This Fastback belonged to a fast-response medical team, but had acquired some non-standard wheel trims by the time it was photographed.

BUYING AND OWNING AN 800

The Rover 800 has been slow to attract a 'classic' following, and as a result large numbers have been scrapped when they could realistically have been resuscitated by somebody who wanted the car as more than simple transport from A to B. This does mean that the choice of examples for sale is now more limited than it might have been, but it also means that most of the really bad examples are no longer around to tempt the unwary buyer.

The 800 range was designed as a luxury car, and many examples (particularly of the more expensive models) were very well maintained by buyers to whom the expense was not a problem. So it is still possible to find very good examples for sale, with complete service histories. However, these are few and far between.

When buying an 800, the basic choice lies between the first-generation (sometimes called 'Mk I') and the second-

Memorabilia of interest to enthusiasts:
the early cars came with a cassette tape
that explained their driving controls.

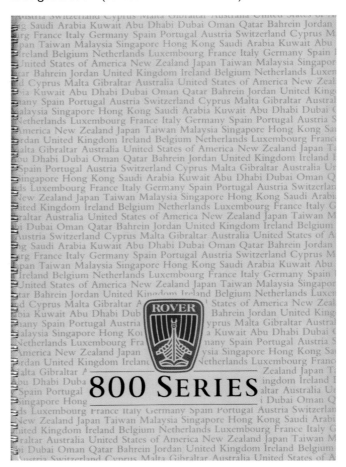

The original 1986 press pack is a rare find today.

This was the cover of a special folder containing sample advertisement blanks for dealers to use in their local newspapers.

The real beauty of it

is the new 2.7 litre engine.

BELOW: **The Rover 800 was regularly included in full-range sales brochures with other Austin Rover models. These are relatively inexpensive to buy from specialist dealers.**

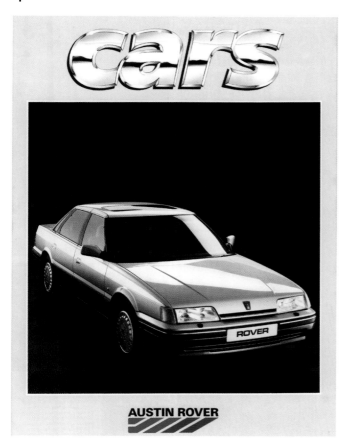

generation (sometimes called 'Mk 2') cars. Some enthusiasts find the 1986–91 cars rather anonymous-looking, while others believe that the more curvaceous later models lost their purity. There is no correct answer to this: it is a matter of taste. However, it is worth noting that the 1992 and later models generally have more opulent interiors and a higher level of equipment than their forebears. Most commentators have also found their handling slightly less crisp, with the notable exception of the Vitesse Sport variants.

Generally speaking, the 800 was designed as a luxury saloon rather than a sports saloon, and most examples show a bias towards ride comfort rather than handling. However, the driving dynamics are good overall for a large car with front-wheel drive. Anyone who puts a premium on performance is likely to be most content with a post-1991 Vitesse (180PS/178bhp) or Vitesse Sport (200PS/197bhp), or with a 1991-model 820 Turbo 16v (180PS/178bhp). The earlier Vitesse with its Honda V6 is rather ordinary, despite the promise of its name. A buyer who wants rarity above all else should probably begin by looking at examples of the 820 Turbo 16v or the Coupé – although the latter tends to polarize opinions.

Most cars for sale are likely to be 2-litre models of one type or another, and all the 2-litre engines have a reputation for reliability. The Honda V6 is also an extremely

147

Another full-range Austin Rover sales brochure, this time promoting the then-new 827SLi model.

four wheel arches, they do not prevent rust altogether. The door bottoms can also rust, especially if drain holes have become blocked, but rust in the frames is not easy to see without lying on the ground and looking up at them from underneath.

It is also worth checking the sunroof aperture for rust, and to see if the drain tubes are doing their job properly; when drain tubes become blocked or perforated, the rainwater has to go somewhere, and may well set up corrosion inside the body sections. The leading edge of the bonnet also suffers badly, mainly because stone chips expose the metal underneath.

Front wings bolt on, and so can be removed for remedial work or replaced altogether if new old-stock panels are available. The rear wings are part of the body structure and have to be repaired in place, which is more difficult and is best left to an expert.

It is wise to look for rust on the 1992 and later cars in all the same places, but these cars had better underseal and paint from new, and most of the rust traps had been eliminated. Although a well-cared-for example of these later cars should have fewer structural problems, it is as well not to assume that it will not have any at all.

A non-structural problem associated with the body is that the exterior door handles often fail. The locating lug on the inside, which is part of the door handle moulding, snaps off so that the handle no longer operates the link to the door catch. Repair is tricky, and replacement with a good second-hand item is generally more realistic.

reliable engine, although the earlier 2.5-litre type can be a little frenzied when worked hard, and the greater torque spread of the later 2.7-litre engine makes a big improvement.

BODY STRUCTURE

Even though rust prevention on cars was generally pretty good by the middle of the 1980s, the early 800s are prone to quite bad corrosion. The obvious signs will probably be on the outer sills and around the rear wheel arches, and severe rusting here should warn of worse problems in less visible areas. It is important to check the rear wheel arches when the back doors are open, and the outer wheel arch on the driver's side in particular is prone to rusting where it meets the rear bumper. Even though there are inner liners in all

ENGINES

Although most of the engines in the 800 range were 2-litre types, there were several different versions over the years. Least powerful was the 100PS (99bhp) carburettor M8 in the 820 Fastback, which was not made in large numbers. Next up came the 120PS (118bhp) M16 with throttle-body injection (in the 'e' models) and the 140PS (138bhp) M16 with multi-point injection (in the 'i' models). There was also a 180PS (178bhp) turbocharged M16 in the short-lived 820 Turbo 16v.

The later T16 engines came in three forms. In standard form with multi-point injection, they had 136PS (134bhp). In turbocharged form for the 1992-on Vitesse, they had 180PS (178bhp), and from May 1994 for the Vitesse Sport they had 200PS (197bhp).

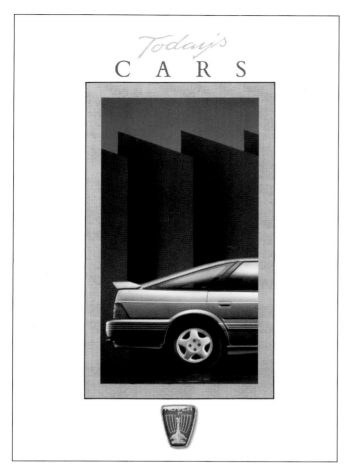

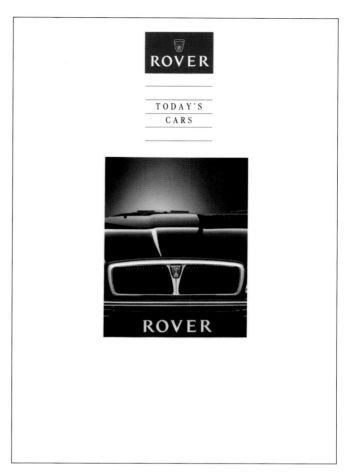

Austin Rover gave their full-range brochures the title of 'Today's Cars' for a number of years. They embraced different styles over those years.

The Honda V6 came as a 2.5-litre with 173PS (171bhp) – or 167PS (165bhp) on automatics – in the early 825 models and as a 2.7-litre with 177PS (175bhp) in the later cars. With a catalytic converter in the exhaust, as was standard from 1992, peak power dropped to 169PS (167bhp). The final V6 engines, from 1996, were Rover's own KV6 types, with 175PS (173bhp). Worth noting at the outset is that the character of all the V6 engines was quite different from that of the 4-cylinders, despite the similarity of power outputs in some cases.

Not to be forgotten are the 118PS (116bhp) diesel engines, which differ slightly between early cars and the post-1992 models.

Little needs to be said about the carburettor-fed M8 engine, which is robust and reliable, and is generally similar to the O-series engine in the far more common Montego and Maestro models. However, it is not an engine to be recommended without some qualification. It left the relatively heavy 820 Fastback feeling somewhat underpowered, and so owners often thrashed it to get the performance they wanted. When treated like this, it not only compromises refinement (creating a great deal of thrash and body boom) but can also suffer premature wear.

The M16 and T16 engines have a lot in common, but a particular point to remember on the M16 types with throttle-body injection is that the ECU will lose its memory if the battery has been disconnected without a trickle charge being applied, and can only be reprogrammed by a dealer with the correct equipment. So when buying, ensure that the battery is connected and that the engine is running as it should. On the M16s with multi-point injection, the air flow meter is a known weakness, but the battery can be disconnected without causing a problem.

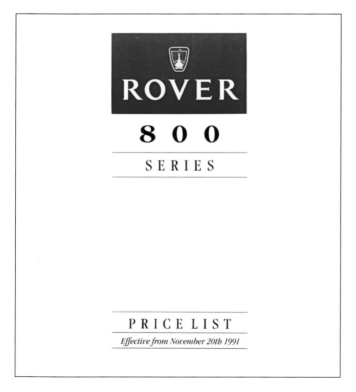

Not all sales brochures for the 800 are very exciting – but items like this contain useful information for the enthusiast.

The O-series, M16 and T16 engines all leak oil from the head-to-block joint at the front right of the engine (as seen with the bonnet open), close to number four cylinder. The leak can vary from seepage to a quite serious flow; in the latter case, check the oil level on the dipstick. The only long-term solution is to replace the head gasket, but sealing in this area is always questionable and the new gasket may well start to leak soon after being fitted. On 1996 and later T16 engines, the tolerances for the head and block faces were tightened and a new multi-layer steel head gasket (made by Klinger) was used. These later engines should suffer less from the problem as a result.

The Klinger gasket can be used on earlier engines, and its presence is detected by a small rectangular piece of gasket protruding from the head-to-block joint near the distributor cap, under the end of the rocker cover. However, without the improved head and block tolerances, the Klinger gasket is not on its own a guarantee that these engines will remain leak-free.

All the 2-litre engines used a rubber belt for the camshaft drive, and this must be changed every 24,000 miles (38,500km). Failure to change the belt can lead to accelerated wear, and a broken or jumped timing belt causes extensive mayhem within the engine. It is therefore vital to check when the belt was last changed – and to ask for proof in the shape of a service receipt.

All the 4-cylinder petrol engines may also have exhaust manifold leaks. The reason is usually that the manifold has been taken off and then refitted using the original studs and nuts. A good clean of the joint face, a new gasket and new studs and nuts will usually cure the problem.

The earliest T16 engines sometimes suffered from sticking valves when cold, and in bad cases the valves would also stick when the engine had reached operating temperature. The result was a persistent misfire. The problem was mainly confined to cars used only for short journeys, and was caused by carbon build-up around the valve stem that hindered movement within the valve guide. Some cars were retrofitted by Rover dealers with carbon valves, and from late 1994 or 1995 these valves were fitted with new guides on the assembly lines as standard. Note that another common cause of misfiring is a warped cylinder head caused by overheating: the warping causes the valve seats to move in relation to the valve guides, so preventing the valves from closing properly.

All these problems also apply to the turbocharged M16 and T16 engines. Those engines are generally robust in other

ROVER
8 0 0
Coupe

Rover's new flagship has no rival.
A car of grace, power and authority, well
worthy of the most discerning driver

**The Coupé was promoted through a number
of sales brochures unique to the model.**

respects but can develop problems with their ECUs and associated control systems.

The two Honda V6 engines are exceptionally reliable, but often develop tappet noise. This is not necessarily serious. If this occurs only when the engine is cold and the oil still thick, it may be no more than air bubbles in the oil; changing the oil will probably cure it, although in persistent cases it may be necessary to change the tappets themselves.

Unexplained coolant loss from the Honda V6 can result from wear of the water pump shaft. This allows coolant to leak onto the engine, where heat causes it to evaporate, so leaving no evidence of where the coolant is going. It is not advisable to leave this problem unchecked for too long because the water pump is driven by the cam belt and, if it seizes, will cause mechanical mayhem in the engine.

The cam belt itself needs to be changed every 46,000 miles (74,000km), a figure later revised to 90,000 (145,000km) by Rover. As with the 4-cylinder engines, check when the work

was last done and ask to see proof. For safety, it is probably best to rely on the earlier recommendation for more frequent cam-belt changes.

Additional Honda V6 problems include a high idling speed. This was often caused by an air lock in the cooling system (typically created when a hose was replaced), which caused the cold-engine/fast-idle system to remain active.

The Rover KV6 engine is unfortunately a very different kettle of fish. Although later versions of this engine were very reliable, the early examples in the 800 Series were built on what was really a low-volume pilot production line and were prone to several maladies. The major one was head-gasket failure, and a check of the oil for 'mayonnaise' under the filler cap is essential when buying a car with one of these engines.

Finally, the diesels are remarkably robust engines, although relatively little known in the UK. Earlier versions of the VM engine were prone to head-gasket problems, but these are fairly uncommon on the versions used in the 800 range. Perhaps the most common problems are with turbocharger bearings: owners often failed to let the turbocharger stop spinning before turning the engine off, so allowing the bearings to be starved of oil and causing rapid wear.

On all cars, a blowing exhaust is a reason for negotiating a price reduction, but it is important to bear in mind that some exhaust sections can be quite expensive. This is particularly true of the front section for the Honda V6 engines, but even more so for the later type with a catalytic converter. Generally speaking, all exhausts with catalytic converters are expensive (by exhaust standards), and it is important to listen carefully for a rattle from the 'cat', which is one of the signs that it has failed and needs to be replaced.

GEARBOXES

The PG1 and PG2 manual gearboxes often develop bearing noise, which is usually an irritation rather than a serious problem – unless the noise is really bad, of course. Repair is not enormously expensive. The differential bearings (the differential is in the gearbox sump) may also wear on cars used hard or not regularly serviced. Otherwise, the usual checks for clutch travel and clutch slip will reveal any problems with a manual 800. The T650 and T750 manual gearboxes used in the diesel models are not known to have any major failings.

There were three types of automatic gearbox. These

were the ZF used with the 4-cylinder petrol engines, the Honda type (later ones with electronic control) with that company's V6 engines, and the JATCO type used with the Rover KV6 engine. As with all automatic gearboxes, a check of the oil can be revealing: black oil or a burnt smell indicate problems. Smooth changes are to be expected, and rough ones indicate problems.

Some ZF gearboxes have suffered from flexi-plate failure, which is detectable through excess slip during changes and is expensive to repair. The Honda gearboxes are generally reliable, although it is important to fill them with the correct Hondamatic oil. The road-speed sensor in the transmission, which sends signals to the speedometer, can also fail.

OBVIOUSLY, WE DON'T BELIEVE EVERYONE SHOULD BE DRIVING A ROVER 800.

Car crime is a major problem. One that every car company is trying to overcome.

And each year, to show how much they have achieved, car makers compete for the BVRLA's* Anti Theft Award.

This year the judges voted unanimously in favour of the Rover 800 Series.

To win the Award, we not only had to beat other car makers.

We also had to prove we could help beat the car thief.

THE NEW ROVER 800 SERIES

 ROVER FLEET   FOR FURTHER INFORMATION CONTACT ROVER CARS FLEET SALES ON 0203 670111. *BRITISH VEHICLE RENTAL AND LEASING ASSOCIATION.

Old advertisements for the Rover 800 have their own charm as collector's pieces.

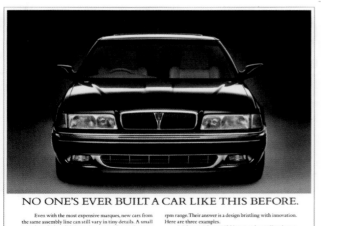

NO ONE'S EVER BUILT A CAR LIKE THIS BEFORE.

Even with the most expensive marques, new cars from the same assembly line can still vary in tiny details. A small gap where the boot lid closes. An extra millimetre between a door and a pillar. Normal discrepancies in normal car manufacture. And the reason why rattles develop over time. Why weather insulation isn't quite perfect. Why the driver's door doesn't slam as crisply as it should.

Stealth bomber technology.

Now Rover have the answer. Before making the car, make a template from graphite. Precise as a cut diamond. Impervious to temperature changes. Accurate to a staggering 0.15mm (the thickness of two human hairs). Now check the car against this perfect template. Exposing the slightest deviation from the designer's original computer model. The same technology is used in the manufacture of the stealth bomber.

A brain that can tell whether you're going to the office or to the golf club.

The new "T"series engine has a huge brain called MEMS (Modular Engine Management System) which continually monitors not only its own performance but also yours. 256 separate pieces of information are received, 40,000 instructions per second are sent; controlling everything that can affect optimum performance – from the angle of your toe to the setting of the air conditioning". (Intelligently, this information is also stored and updated; making servicing shorter, cheaper and more efficient.)

The ultimate challenge: low speed torque plus high speed power.

The brief to Rover engineers was for an engine of effortless power especially in the all-important 2,000 to 3,500

rpm range. Their answer is a design bristling with innovation. Here are three examples.

1. A longer inlet manifold tract and a smaller plenum chamber giving an increased "Ram Air"effect at lower speeds – thus better low speed torque.

2. An advanced "internal breathing" cylinder block and head eliminating the need for a complex external system and improving running, oil consumption and emissions.

3. A unique sump design which reduces noise and vibration by –2db. (That may not sound much but here, as everywhere, refinement is the key.)

Walnut, leather.... and fingertip control.

Walnut, up to one hundred years old, crafted and curved to produce a driving environment that is pure Rover. Connolly hides,'tanned with sumac leaves, mimosa bark and myrobalan. Carpeting to sink your toes into.

Yet every piece of state-of-the-art ingenuity is at your fingertips. Infra-red lazy locking. A doubly sophisticated ultra-sonic alarm system which not only senses changes in internal air pressure but also reacts to a voltage drop caused by an opening door, bonnet or boot.

A catalyst as standard. Also available are a CD auto-changer and blissful air conditioning.

There are many pleasures to owning the new Rover 800. Not least is the knowledge that at last you can drive a European quality car built *precisely* as the designer intended.

THE NEW ROVER 800 SERIES

IT LOOKS EVEN MORE ATTRACTIVE WHEN PLACED ON THE BALANCE SHEET.

Luxury without largesse. Fiscal responsibility without personal deprivation. Even the most difficult of Managing Directors (or Financial Directors) would approve.

THE NEW ROVER 800 SERIES

FOR FURTHER INFORMATION CONTACT ROVER CARS FLEET SALES ON 0265 670111.

These 1992 advertisements were aimed particularly at fleet buyers.

The JATCO gearbox is – theoretically – sealed for life, although many owners take the precaution of changing the oil once in a while. Note that some brands of the special synthetic oil used in this gearbox are very expensive. Other faults with the JATCO gearbox are typically attributable to failed sensors in the electronic control system.

INTERIOR AND ELECTRICAL EQUIPMENT

There are few interior problems with 800s. Seats wear well, although light-coloured leather upholstery usually shows its age first. The switchgear on first-generation cars can sometimes be fragile, especially the switches for the wipers and the headlamps. Interior door handles on early cars can also

break, and their rather flimsy return springs can snap and allow the handle to flap around.

The heater control panel has a couple of contacts that eventually wear and are expensive to replace. However, they can usually be bent into shape again after dismantling the dashboard to gain access. The ball connection in the wiper mechanism can also shear, but can be repaired easily enough by drilling it and fitting a self-tapping screw.

Electric windows may give trouble on 800s of all ages, but the problem is often nothing worse than dry joints on the fuse box circuit board, and can be easily put right by resoldering. The later cars with a greater profusion of electrical equipment may give more trouble, simply because there is more to go wrong. Trip computers may play up, alarms may go off without reason when the car is parked, and immobilizers can sometimes make a car refuse to start at the most inconvenient moment. Most of these problems are caused by faulty sensors or micro-switches, but sometimes need a good deal of determination to track down. The more electrical equipment there is on a car, the more imperative it is to check everything during a test drive.

The 1996 and later cars had a four-figure immobilizer code that could be used to deactivate the immobilizer in an emergency. It is important to make sure the code is with the car (it is usually among the owner's documents) because if the remote key fob fails, it will be impossible to start the car without it.

SUSPENSION, STEERING AND BRAKES

The 800's suspension was set up for ride comfort rather than sharp handling, although the tuned system fitted to the Vitesse Sport altered the bias considerably. Many of the pre-facelift versions of the more expensive models had self-levelling rear suspension, which is useful when towing a trailer or caravan but can fail after a time. The correct replacement dampers were discontinued some years ago, but it is possible to replace them with standard (non-level-ling) dampers as long as the road springs are changed at the same time.

All 800s have one type or another of variable-ratio steer-ing. The 4-cylinder and KV6 cars use Rover's own PCF sys-tem, and the Honda-engined cars use that company's own speed-variable system. Both are very light in operation, although the PCF system feels more positive. Groaning noises from the steering indicate hydraulic problems (such as low fluid or a failed pump), while knocking noises indicate mechanical faults in the linkages.

Brakes give excellent stopping power and were regu-larly praised in road tests when the cars were new. A slightly soft feel to the pedal is normal. The front brakes have a wear sensor, but only on one side. As pads can wear unevenly, it is therefore possible for those on the side without the sensor to wear right down to bare metal before the other side triggers the wear warning light. Squealing brakes should always be investigated, if only for this reason.

Cars with ABS have a warning light on the dash. This should light up as a check when the ignition is switched on, but should then go out. If it stays on, there is probably a fault

with one of the sensors. Faults like this are potentially safety critical and are best left to a specialist rather than tackled on the driveway at home.

On a car that has been unused for some time, it is advisable to make sure that the handbrake releases prop-erly, as the cams for the mechanism in the rear calipers can seize.

CLUBS AND SPECIALISTS

The Rover 800 has been supported for a long time by dedicated enthusiasts who have provided helpful owner information on the internet. There have been too many

This advertisement was one of the first ever issued for the Rover 800, in July 1986.

sites to list here, some more useful than others, but a search for 'Rover 800 problems' will normally turn up the most prominent ones. At long last, in November 2015, a proper Rover 800 Owners' Club was formed. At the time of writing, its website was still being established, but the club could be contacted by e-mail on rover800ownersclub@ gmail.com. In addition, the Rover Sports Register, which caters for Rovers of all ages, welcomes 800 owners; its website is www.thersr.co.uk.

As for parts and specialists, suppliers change over time and it would potentially be misleading to give details here. An exception, however, may be made for the leading suppliers of Rover 800 parts. Rimmer Brothers, based in Lincoln, can be contacted through their website, www.rimmerbros.co.uk.

ROVER 800 WHEEL STYLES

By the time the Rover 800 was introduced, wheel design had become an important element in the overall design of a car. The more upmarket models always had alloy wheels, and at least some of these alloys were available on the less expensive models. These lower-priced cars generally came with steel disc wheels and styled polycarbonate wheel trims.

Rover publicity material very often pictured cars with optional alloy wheels, not least because these made the less expensive models look more desirable. It is therefore quite difficult to determine from this material exactly what the 'standard' wheel designs were.

What follows is an attempt to make sense of the multiple wheel designs that were available on the Rover 800 models between 1986 and 1998.

1987–1988 model-years

ABOVE LEFT: **Entry-level models (820i and 820E) had steel disc wheels with these 'pepperpot' trims.**

ABOVE CENTRE: **The next models up the range, 820SE and 820Si, again had steel wheels as standard, but with these wheel trims.**

ABOVE RIGHT: **These were the alloy wheels, standard on the Sterling and optional on the 825i.**

LEFT: **For 1988, the Sterling switched to the cross-spoke alloy wheels previously available only on the US models (albeit with different centre badges).**

1989 model year

FAR LEFT: **These attractive five-spoke alloy wheels arrived in May 1988 as standard wear for the Vitesse.**

LEFT: **A unique five-spoke alloy wheel was available to go with the new body styling kit. It was later made available as the Roversport type.**

1990–1991 model years

ABOVE LEFT: **Entry-level models came with steel wheels as standard, and with this design of wheel trim, which matched one used on the new 200 range.**

ABOVE CENTRE: **This was the new wheel trim for the 820i.**

ABOVE RIGHT: **At SL trim level, there was yet another new style of alloy wheel.**

BOTTOM LEFT: **The original style of Roversport five-spoke alloy wheel had a groove around the hub section but no Rover badge. It was used unchanged on some Sterling models for the USA.**

BOTTOM RIGHT: **When the Roversport alloy wheel was no longer needed to do duty on the US-model Sterlings, it was modified to incorporate a central Rover emblem. The revised style also lost the groove around the hub.**

1992–1995 model years

ABOVE LEFT: **There was yet another style of wheel trim for the steel wheels on entry-level and S models.**

ABOVE CENTRE: **This was the six-spoke alloy wheel for the SL models from the 1992 model year.**

ABOVE RIGHT: **The Vitesse meanwhile went over to this seven-spoke alloy design, which would also be used on S and SL models from 1995.**

BOTTOM LEFT: **This fifteen-hole alloy wheel design was adopted for the 1992 model-year Sterling and remained standard on that model until the end of production. It was known as the Prestige type.**

BOTTOM RIGHT: **With the Vitesse Sport came a new six-spoke alloy wheel.**

1996–1998 model years

For the 1996 season, this style of alloy wheel was fitted to both **S** and **SL** level models. Though similar to the style used on the Vitesse, it lacked the indentations around the centre.

IDENTIFICATION CODES FOR ROVER 800s

VIN codes

The VIN (Vehicle Identification Number) of a Rover 800 is stamped on a plate secured to the lower left-hand centre door pillar. It consists of a seventeen-character alphanumeric string. The first eleven characters provide details of the specification, and the final six digits are a serial number.

The eleven-character prefix breaks down as follows:

SAX   Rover Group UK (manufacturer code)

XS   800 Series to 1991 (basic range code)
- RS   800 Series from 1992 model year

C   Sterling or Coupé (class code)
- H   820i, 825D or 827i
- S   820Si, 820SLi, 820TI, 825SD, 825SLD, 827Si or 827SLi
- W   Vitesse
- Y   820 Turbo

L   Four-door saloon (body type code)
- C   Two-door Coupé
- W   Five-door Fastback

C   2.5-litre diesel (engine code)
- D   2-litre Mpi LTi
- F   2-litre Mpi turbo (180PS)
- G   2.7-litre V6 non-catalyst
- K   2.7-litre V6 with catalyst
- L   2.5-litre KV6
- V   2-litre Mpi turbo (200PS)
- W   2-litre Mpi LTi non-catalyst

D   Five-speed manual PG2, RHD (gearbox and steering code)
- B   Five-speed PG1 uprated, RHD (820 Turbo)
- E   Five-speed A568, RHD
- F   Five-speed PG1, RHD
- G   Five-speed uprated PG1, RHD
- J   Four-speed ZF automatic, RHD
- K   Four-speed JATCO automatic, RHD
- L   Four-speed EAT automatic, RHD
- M   Five-speed PG1, LHD for France
- P   Five-speed PG2, LHD
- R   Five-speed A568, LHD
- S   Five-speed PG1, LHD
- T   Five-speed uprated PG1, LHD
- X   Four-speed ZF automatic, LHD
- Z   Four-speed EAT automatic, LHD
- N/K Four-speed JATCO automatic, LHD

A   Model year or change

M   Built at Cowley

Serial Number

Sample six-digit serial numbers, mostly taken from service literature, are as follows. Note that many numbers used on pre-1992 models were reused on post-1992 models – the alphanumeric prefix would of course have been different.

170190	Last 2.5-litre V6 model, February 1988
177133	First UK-market 820 Fastback, May 1988
179968	First UK-market Vitesse, May 1988
200605	October 1988
244247	October 1989
276672	September 1990
296949	1991 820 Turbo
100318	First RS coded car, October 1991 (1992 model year)
152091	First 1993 model
194917	First 1994 model
230967	First 1996 model, January 1996
242827	First 1997 model
260898	Final Rover 800, September 1998

A full list of engine codes was not available at press time. What follows is therefore a partial list.

2-litre petrol engines

On early engines, the engine number is found stamped into a plate attached to the cylinder block sump flange, behind the exhaust down-pipe. On later engines, the number is in a dot-matrix marking on the cylinder block above the right-hand core plug.

These engines are identified by the prefix code 20T. There are three alphanumeric groups in the full eight-character prefix code, which is followed by a six-digit serial number. An example of a full engine code is 20T4HF82-100101. (Note that the hyphen has been inserted for clarity here and does not appear on the identification plate.) The full prefix code can be interpreted as follows:

20T 2-litre, T-series engine
4 4v per cylinder
H Long-track injection, normally aspirated
  G = Long-track injection, turbocharged
F82 Multi-point long-track injection with R4DT type manual gearbox
F84 Multi-point long-track injection with air conditioning and R4DT type manual gearbox
F86 Multi-point long-track injection with automatic gearbox
F88 Multi-point long-track injection with air conditioning and automatic gearbox
G10 Multi-point long-track injection with turbocharger and W4DT type manual gearbox
G11 Multi-point long-track injection with turbocharger, air conditioning and W4DT type manual gearbox
G26 Multi-point long-track injection with V4DT type manual gearbox
G27 Multi-point long-track injection with air conditioning and V4DT type manual gearbox
G69 Multi-point long-track injection with Lucas injectors, CFC-free air conditioning and R4DT type manual gearbox
G70 Multi-point long-track injection with Lucas injectors, CFC-free air conditioning and V4DT type manual gearbox
G71 Multi-point long-track injection with Lucas injectors, CFC-free air conditioning and automatic gearbox

G72 Multi-point long-track injection with Lucas injectors, turbocharger (180PS), CFC-free air conditioning and W4DT type manual gearbox
G78 Multi-point long-track injection with Lucas injectors and R4DT type manual gearbox
G79 Multi-point long-track injection with Lucas injectors and V4DT type manual gearbox
G80 Multi-point long-track injection with Lucas injectors and automatic gearbox
G81 Multi-point long-track injection with Lucas injectors, turbocharger (180PS) and W4DT type manual gearbox
H04 Multi-point long-track injection with Lucas injectors, turbocharger (200PS) and W4DTUT type manual gearbox
H05 Multi-point long-track injection with Lucas injectors, turbocharger (200PS), CFC-free air conditioning and W4DTUT type manual gearbox
H16 Multi-point long-track injection with Lucas injectors, CFC-free air conditioning and automatic gearbox
H20 Multi-point long-track injection with Lucas injectors and automatic gearbox
H33 Multi-point long-track injection with Lucas injectors, turbocharger (200PS) and W4DTUT type manual gearbox
H34 Multi-point long-track injection with Lucas injectors, turbocharger (200PS), CFC-free air conditioning and W4DTUT type manual gearbox
H39 Stripped engine, LBB 10465
H40 Stripped engine, LBB 10467
H41 Stripped engine, LBB 10464
H42 Stripped engine, LBB 10466
H50 Stripped engine, LBB 10468
H51 Stripped engine, LBB 10469
H93 Multi-point long-track injection with Lucas injectors, CFC-free air conditioning, 1994 (May) immobilization and R4DT type manual gearbox
H94 Multi-point long-track injection with Lucas injectors, CFC-free air conditioning, 1994 (May) immobilization and V4DT type manual gearbox
H95 Multi-point long-track injection with Lucas injectors, turbocharger (180PS), CFC-free air conditioning, 1994 (May) immobilization and W4DT type manual gearbox
H96 Multi-point long-track injection with Lucas injectors, 1994 (May) immobilization and R4DT type manual gearbox

H97   Multi-point long-track injection with Lucas injectors, 1994 (May) immobilization and V4DT type manual gearbox

H98   Multi-point long-track injection with Lucas injectors, turbocharger (180PS), 1994 (May) immobilization and W4DT type manual gearbox

2.5-litre turbocharged diesel engines

The engine number is stamped into the cylinder block just below the high-pressure pipes at the rear of the injection pump. These engines all have a prefix code of 97A, followed by a five-digit serial number, such as 97A-01234. (Note that the hyphen has been inserted for clarity here and does not appear on the identification plate.)

2.7-litre Honda V6 engines

The engine number is stamped on the block behind the front timing-belt cover. There are two basic types of these engines, each with a five-character identifying prefix and a seven-digit serial number. The types are as follows:

C27A1 with serial   7000001 with catalytic
numbers from   converter
C27A2   7600001 without catalytic
                         converter

ROVER 800 PRODUCTION FIGURES

At the time of writing, detailed production records had been found only for a small proportion of all the Rover 800s built. However, it seems clear that a total of 317,126 cars were built, and that the calendar-year figures break down like this:

Year	Figure	
1986	15,609	
1987	54,434	
1988	48,634	
1989	35,387	
1990	29,460	
1991 (pre-facelift)	10,007	
1991 (post-facelift)	2,961	(1991 total: 12,968)
1992	28,136	
1993	28,354	
1994	21,802	
1995	13,311	
1996	11,400	
1997	11,131	
1998	6,500	

THE 800 OVERSEAS

The number of overseas markets where the 800 range was sold varied over the years but was generally between twenty-five and thirty. In the 1987 calendar year, for example, Rover claimed to have sold examples in twenty-seven overseas markets. The start of sales in some of these had been delayed until the second quarter of 1987, when a European version of the V6 engine with catalytic converter that had been primarily developed for the USA allowed a start to sales in Austria, Germany and Switzerland. This was previewed at the Geneva Show in March 1987.

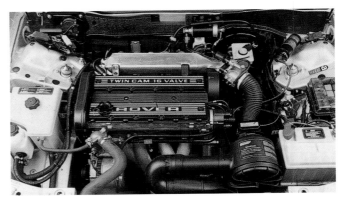

This is the underbonnet view of an M16i engine in a left-hand-drive car. Compare this with the picture of a right-hand-drive car in Chapter 2.

In May 1988, the 800 saloons were being exported to 'over twenty' countries, and by June 1988 the range (including Fastbacks) was on sale in twenty-six countries, a figure that had risen to thirty by the end of August that year. Exports of the facelifted models appear to have begun in March 1992 with France, Germany and Spain, followed in April by cars for Belgium Holland, Italy and other overseas markets.

What follows are snapshots of the Rover 800 in a number of markets outside the UK. More research is needed to establish a fuller picture.

Australia

Jaguar Rover Australia imported only V6-engined models of the 800 range between 1987 and 1991. One early Sterling was imported for evaluation, but JRA considered that it would be too expensive for the local market and decided instead on a two-model range. So the Australian range initially consisted of the 825Si and 825Si Special models, the former available with either manual or automatic gearbox,

Looking a little unfamiliar to UK eyes, this is the dashboard of a left-hand-drive Sterling dating from 1988.

Rover enthusiasts swarm around the 825 Sterling evaluation model at the importer's premises during 1986. The company eventually decided not to take the top-model 800.

the latter coming as standard with leather upholstery, rear headrests and the automatic gearbox.

When the enlarged 2.7-litre V6 engine became available during 1988, the model range was revised to become 827Si and Sterling. The 827Si was available with either manual or automatic gearbox, while the Sterling came with metallic paint and contrasting lower panels, alloy wheels, leather upholstery with rear head restraints, and automatic as standard. The 827 Vitesse in Fastback form was then added to the range during 1989, with automatic as the only gearbox option. The final revisions came in 1990, when the 827Si model was discontinued and a new three-model range was

made available, consisting of the Sterling saloon, the 827 Fastback and the 827 Vitesse (the latter again being a Fastback).

Two factors contributed to the demise of the 800 range in Australia. One was unfavourable currency exchange rates, and the other was a decision by the Australian Federal Government to increase the tax on luxury cars from 30 per cent to 50 per cent from 1 April 1990. So Rover Australia (as the importing company had become) stopped importing Rover cars to focus on importing and distributing Land Rovers, Land Rover Discoverys and Range Rovers. The facelifted R17 and R18 models were therefore never imported commercially, and no Rover cars were available in Australia until February 2001, when imports of the new Rover 75 models began.

Austria

The Austrian cars were required to have an exhaust emissions control system with catalytic converter. Sales here did not begin until V6 models with that specification became available in the second quarter of 1987.

France

Austin Rover France announced the 800 range at the Paris Motor Show in October 1986. There were four models – the 820i, 820Si, 825i Sterling and 825i Sterling with an option pack (which consisted of ABS, leather upholstery, two-tone

The French market became a major one for Austin Rover. Austin Rover France took its own press pictures – these two show an early 820i.

and the end of 1988, all of the Rover 800s sold in Japan were actually built on the Honda assembly lines at Sayama. As Chapter 2 explains, they had a number of differences from the UK-built cars. After December 1988, all 800s for Japan were assembled in the UK.

The 800s sold in Japan were generally very well equipped and were sold as luxury models. Later models included a very highly specified version of the Coupé, with 2.7-litre Honda V6 engine.

Malta

The 800 range was available in Malta by summer 1988.

Netherlands

The Dutch were keen Rover buyers, and took the 820i, 820Si and Sterling models from 1986. Austin Rover Nederland approved both an LPG (Liquefied Petroleum Gas) conversion and a pair of aftermarket body kits from the summer of 1987.

Many European countries favoured the leather option for the Sterling. This is a Dutch-market car.

New Zealand

New Zealand was an early export market for the 800, because it was able to take cars with the same specification as those sold on the UK market. The range was launched in summer 1987, early models being the 820Si in manual form, 825i automatic and 825 Sterling. There was no special publicity when the 2.7-litre V6 models arrived in 1988, probably because there were still unsold stocks of the earlier 2.5-litre cars.

An early 820Si for the Dutch market.

New Zealand became the first export market for Fast-back models, when 820i and Vitesse derivatives were displayed at the Auckland Show in July 1988. There were still examples of the 825Si around in September 1989, when the car was listed with either manual or automatic gearbox alongside the 827SLi automatic. Other models available at this stage were the 820Si manual (saloon or Fastback), 820SE automatic (also saloon or Fastback), and Vitesse with either manual or automatic gearbox.

The 800 Series was always expensive in New Zealand, and the cars were slow sellers at a time when the local economy was not buoyant. When the New Zealand government abolished restrictions on imported second-hand cars in the late 1980s, the market was flooded with high-specification models from Japan and Singapore, which did nothing for the sales of new 800s.

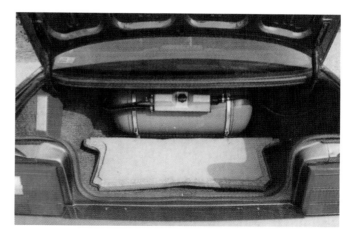

The Dutch were keen on LPG systems in the 1980s. Austin Rover Nederland approved this Landi-Hartog conversion for the 800 Series early on.

The Dutch were not slow to develop body kits for the 800, and this one by Interstate Europe BV in Delft gained approval from Austin Rover Nederland in mid-1987. The suspension has been lowered, and there are aftermarket 14in alloy wheels with 6in rims. There are side stripes, in this case with an 820i decal on the rear wing, and a boot-lid spoiler.

Austin Rover Nederland also approved this body kit, which became available through selected dealers. Again, the suspension has been lowered and there are aftermarket alloy wheels with low-profile tyres. A special front spoiler and boot-lid spoiler are matched by Sterling-style dark lower panels; there is also a wind deflector for the sunroof. This one cost 11,000 guilders in mid-1987.

The second-generation cars were exported to New Zealand, and publicity for the 1993 model year talked about the 'return of Rover'. That publicity referred to the 827 Sterling and to the 800 Coupé, although in practice the Coupé seems not to have been imported.

The Rover importers focused more on less expensive models from the 200 and 400 ranges, and there were few imports of the KV6-engined 825 models as new cars. The main dealer in Auckland, for example, sold just three (all in 1997). However, many KV6 models did reach New Zealand as second-hand imports from Japan. That same Auckland dealer handled twenty-three such cars. Another example concerns a batch of twenty, all with blown engines, brought in from Japan in late 2000 by a company in Christchurch. The workshop foreman there remembered that they cost around $NZ2,000 each and that after engine rebuilds they were sold on for between $NZ40,000 and $NZ60,000 each, depending on specification.

(Special thanks to Adrian Chandler for information used here.)

Singapore

The 800 range was available in Singapore by summer 1988.

Switzerland

As was the case in Austria and West Germany, Swiss regulations required an exhaust emissions control system with catalytic converter. Sales therefore did not begin here until V6 models with that specification became available in the second quarter of 1987.

Taiwan

Taiwan was among the markets that were receiving saloon models in May 1988.

USA

The full story of the North American specification cars, which wore Sterling badges, is told in Chapter 5. In 1987, the USA was the biggest single overseas market for 800 derivatives.

EXPORT FIGURES

Although Rover made strenuous efforts to turn the 800 into an export success, the majority of sales were always made on the home market. No precise export figures are available, but it is possible to get an overall picture from figures that Rover Group released in connection with other issues.

The company claimed to have sold more than 23,000 examples outside the UK during the 1987 calendar year. Although that figure is imprecise, it is precise enough to suggest that around 42 per cent of the 800s built that year were exported. Then, with a recall notice for a minor problem in January 1994, came some figures that showed that 51,077 cars had been built between October 1991 and November 1993, of which 32,361 had been sold in the UK. This suggested that 18,716 had been exported, or a figure of around 37 per cent.

THE HONDA LEGEND

By the end of the 1970s, Honda had created a number of small-to-medium sized cars that were selling well on the Japanese domestic market and had also made an impression in Europe and in the USA. The company's obvious next step was to develop a larger, luxury-class car for sale in all these markets, and the deal with Austin Rover (as it then was) provided access to experience and expertise that Honda did not have at that stage.

In the Japanese market, Honda's aim was to attract wealthy middle-aged customers and to steal sales from the established large saloons of the time – the Toyota Crown, the Mazda Luce and the Nissan Cedric and Gloria. In Europe, the company simply wanted to improve its market penetration. In the USA, however, there were special conditions. Honda (along with other Japanese car makers) had agreed to limit car sales by volume under a voluntary restraint system that US trade officials had negotiated as a way of protecting domestic manufacturers. All the Japanese makers affected by this trade agreement realized that a move towards larger cars with larger profit margins would maintain profit levels from fewer sales. In 1986, Honda became the first to create a special luxury brand for the USA, which it called Acura; in 1989, Toyota followed with Lexus, and Nissan with Infiniti.

The new large Honda was therefore marketed under two different names. It was launched at the Tokyo Motor Show on 22 October 1985 as a Honda Legend, but its launch in 1987 onto the North American market saw it being sold as an Acura Legend. As explained in Chapter 2, Honda's advanced production engineering capability enabled the Japanese company to launch its version of the car nine months before the Rover equivalent became available, even though the original plan had been to introduce the two cars simultaneously.

In Japan, three variants of the Honda Legend became available for the 1986 model year. The entry-level model was called the V6Zi, and had a 2-litre V6 engine that was not available in Legends built for export. Above this came the better-equipped V6Gi with the same engine. The dimensions of both these models were carefully trimmed to fit within a Japanese category where buyers paid less tax. The third model, the V6Xi, shared the more luxurious equipment specification of the V6Gi. However, it also had two other important differences. One was its size: it had the extended front and rear bumper covers developed for export models. The other was that it had a more powerful 2.5-litre version of the V6 engine.

All the export models of the Legend had the extended bumper covers and the larger V6 engine, and all were badged as V6-2.5i models. They became available in Europe in autumn 1986, a few months after the Rover 800 was

As introduced in 1985, the Honda Legend was recognizably related to the Rover 800 and yet also quite distinctive. The wheel-arch 'blisters' were a notable and stylish feature, and the 'low nose' look gave the car a strong Honda family resemblance.

The dashboard was quite different from the one used in the Rover. Note in particular the 'satellite' control switches embedded in the rim of the instrument panel.

released; for the USA, the Acura Legend was introduced at about the same time, although in this case it anticipated the Rover's arrival with Sterling badges in North America by some months. With emissions-control equipment to meet US standards, the 2.5-litre V6 engine was rated at 151bhp.

Honda's overall approach was to make as much luxury equipment as possible standard on the cars, although there were variations between markets. A basic choice for all territories was between a five-speed manual and a four-speed automatic gearbox, both of Honda's own manufacture. Air conditioning was an option on the European Legends, and so was a special equipment pack with headlamp wash-wipe, alloy wheels, cruise control, multi-way electric driver's seat adjustment, adjustable rear headrests, and an upgraded ICE system.

PRESS REACTIONS

The Legend was very well received in the USA, where it won *Motor Trend* magazine's Import Car of the Year title for 1987 and went on to win *Car and Driver* magazine's Ten Best category three years in a row. The North American models did not have some of the items used on the Japanese market cars, notably the one-touch automatic climate control and the brown woollen cloth upholstery: only blue was available.

The big Honda was less warmly received in Britain, where there was understandably some special sympathy for the Rover version of the design. *Autocar* magazine tested examples of each back-to-back for its issue dated 15 October 1986, and commented:

> *after about 10 minutes … the ride of the Legend comes into question. It seems to be under-damped in that small irregularities in the road surface are transmitted through the body. The Rover has a far smoother ride.*

The UK-market versions of the Legend were actually built in Britain, alongside Rover versions at the Cowley factory. However, there seem to have been build-quality issues from the start. An article in *The Independent* newspaper of 6 February 1994 reported that few of the Cowley-built Legends passed Honda's stringent quality checks, and that a number of them ended up being used for transport around the factory site. The Legend was certainly not a big success in Britain, and only 4,409 examples were built at Cowley before Honda decided to supply the UK from its own factory at Sayama in Japan from summer 1988.

THE LEGEND COUPÉ

Despite the close engineering cooperation between Honda and Rover during the development period of the Legend, Rover seem to have remained blissfully unaware of Honda's interest in a two-door coupé derivative. So the introduction of a Legend Coupé in February 1987 – at a time when their own plans for a coupé were on hold – caught them by surprise. The car had presumably been developed by a team at Honda's Japanese engineering centre in Tochigi Prefecture once the hard points for the saloon had been signed off.

The Legend Coupé was intended to attract buyers who might otherwise have gone for luxury coupés such as the Jaguar XJ-S or the Mercedes-Benz 300CE. Fully in tune with its coupé name, it sat on a short-wheelbase version of the Legend platform (Rover's 800 Coupé would share the saloon's wheelbase when it was introduced some five years later). The car had a drag coefficient of 0.30 as against the 0.32 of the standard saloon in export form. The Coupé also seems to have had a revised rear suspension from the start: Honda had never really liked the idea of the strut rear sus-

The Legend Coupé was a good-looking design. As these pictures show, its alloy wheels differed from those on the saloons and there was a contrasting band of light grey along the lower body edges to make the car look longer and lower than it was.

The interior of the Legend Coupé was suitably luxurious, although rear-seat legroom was necessarily compromised by the short wheelbase.

pension, and had engineered a new double-wishbone type, which made its bow on the Coupé.

Coupés came only with the larger V6 engine in Japan, and also with the extended bumper covers. They were made available for export as well, and in the USA were sold as Acura Legend Coupés. Examples were exported to Britain (no Legend Coupés were made at Cowley), and *Autocar* magazine tested one against the obvious rivals from Mercedes-Benz and Jaguar for its issue dated 3 February 1988. Although the car was impressive, it was outclassed – not least in terms of maximum speed, which was way below that of the other two cars.

'Despite the modernity of its lean design,' reported *Autocar*, 'the Legend Coupé doesn't make the grade in this company. It's a beautifully-engineered, well-built and stylish car with only minor flaws, but it's not a £24,000 car.' There were good elements: 'The Honda is pleasant and spacious to sit in, there is a bit of wood on the centre console as a

UK PRODUCTION OF THE HONDA LEGEND	
1986	472
1987	2,677
1988	1,260
Total	4,409

sop to sybarites, and in most respects it exudes quality.' However:

> Some things grate for a car of this class, the shiny coarse-grain plastic fabric linings look cheap, the boot lid feels flimsy, and the carpet trimming the large, but shallow luggage area is of poor quality.

Honda still had a lot to learn about luxury cars at this stage.

THE 1988 MODELS

Rover expected their 800 saloon to remain in production for around ten years, so a midlife facelift was scheduled for about 1991 – and indeed the revised R17 Fastback and R18 saloon models appeared that autumn for the 1992 model year. Honda, by contrast, had probably seen the Legend as a short-term expedient from the start. The company was breaking into a new area of the market and no doubt expected to make mistakes, but was clearly prepared to learn from them, and to learn quickly. With an anticipated production life of only around five years (a replacement model was ready by summer 1990), Honda therefore saw the need for revised versions of their car much earlier, and put them into production during the 1988 model year.

The main changes were to the engines. The 2.5-litre V6 engine was completely replaced by a 2.7-litre type that offered improved torque characteristics. (This same new engine, which used the variable inlet manifold pioneered on the 2-litre V6, was also supplied to Rover for the 800 from the start of 1988.) For the Japanese market only, a turbo-charged derivative of the 2-litre V6 engine was added to the range. This had a variable-geometry turbocharger, which was known as the Wing Turbo because of its variable vanes ('wings'). Not only did it boost power beyond that available even from the new 2.7-litre V6, but it also improved fuel efficiency and reduced emissions, so reducing the associated tax payable in Japan. The Wing Turbo came only with an automatic gearbox and in the 'short' Japanese form. It carried a Turbo badge on the lower right of the grille and a V6Ti identifier on the boot lid.

The 1988 model year also brought the option of a more luxurious level of equipment known as 'Exclusive'. Its features included remote keyless entry, chrome-plated power folding mirrors, automatic headlights with a wash-wipe system, and a separate climate control system for rear-seat passengers. Exclusive also brought wood trim for the dashboard and centre console. Honda had not ignored the criticisms that their interiors depended too much on plastics, and they had gone to Tendo Mokko (a fashionable furniture maker based at Tendo, in the Yamagata prefecture) for a selection of wood types and colours.

For 1988, the US-market Acura Legend came with a driver's side airbag as standard equipment, but lost the tilt-adjustable steering column of 1987 models as a result.

THE FINAL CARS

The 1989 model year was the last one for the first-generation Honda Legend, and that year's cars were introduced on 14 October 1988. A major engineering change was to the rear suspension, as saloon models for all markets took on the double-wishbone type that was already standard on the Legend Coupé. This change on the Honda production lines coincided with the end of Rover 800 production in Japan and the end of Honda Legend production at the Rover plant in Cowley. As a result, neither the Japanese-built Rover 800s nor the Cowley-built Honda Legends ever had the new suspension.

This is a late-model Acura Legend. Note the two-piece headlamp units and the special side-lamp cluster incorporating a side running light. IFCAR/WIKIMEDIA

Otherwise, the main change for this final model year was to the dashboard and interior, which was changed in small details to achieve a more luxurious appearance. This was partly to give the cars additional appeal in their final year before the new model arrived, but also to improve their competitiveness against rival models from Toyota and Nissan.

In North America, the Acura Legend was mildly modified with one-piece headlamps (standard on Japanese cars since the beginning), new alloy wheels, and small changes to the front bumper, boot lid and tail lights. There was also a new LS model, which featured burr walnut interior trim.

THE SECOND GENERATION

Once the first-generation Legend and Rover 800 had been launched, both Honda and Rover were free to develop their versions of the design as they saw fit. Honda had begun to do so early on, adding a coupé to the range in 1987 and modifying the rear suspension later that year. The Japanese company rapidly absorbed feedback from all markets where the Legend was sold and by autumn 1990 had a second-generation Legend ready for production.

Introduced on 24 October 1990, the new Legends again included both saloon and coupé types, and once again the range had a planned life of some five years. The KA7 and KA8 models were based on an entirely new platform and came with just one engine, a 3.2-litre V6 known as the C32A type. None of the new Honda technology fed into the Rover 800, which retained the old platform until its production ended in 1996.

TECHNICAL SPECIFICATIONS – HONDA LEGEND (MODELS KAI–KA6, 1985–1990)

Engines

Honda C20A V6 petrol
Aluminium alloy block and cylinder head
1996cc (82 x 63mm)
Single ohc on each cylinder bank
4v per cylinder
Five-bearing crankshaft
Compression ratio 9.6:1
Honda PGM-FI multi-point injection
145PS (143bhp) at 6,300rpm
172Nm (127lb ft) at 5,000rpm

Honda C20AT V6 turbocharged petrol
Aluminium alloy block and cylinder head
1996cc (82 x 63mm)
Single ohc on each cylinder bank
4v per cylinder
Five-bearing crankshaft
Compression ratio 9.6:1
Honda PGM-FI multi-point injection
Variable-vane turbocharger and intercooler
190PS (190bhp) at 6,000rpm
241Nm (178lb ft) at 3,500rpm

Honda C25A V6 petrol (1986 and 1987 model years)
Aluminium alloy block and cylinder head
2494cc (84 x 75mm)
Single ohc on each cylinder bank
4v per cylinder
Five-bearing crankshaft
Compression ratio 9.6:1
Honda PGM-FI multi-point injection
165PS (163bhp) at 6,000rpm (US models 151bhp)
211Nm (156lb ft) at 4,500rpm

Honda C27A V6 petrol (from 1988 model year)
Aluminium alloy block and cylinder head
2675cc (87 x 75mm)
Single ohc on each cylinder bank
4v per cylinder
Four-bearing crankshaft
Compression ratio 9.4:1
Honda PGM-FI multi-point injection
180PS (180bhp) at 6,000rpm (US models 161bhp)
226Nm (167lb ft) at 4,500rpm

Transmission
Five-speed manual gearbox (Honda type PG2)
   Ratios 2.92:1, 1.79:1, 1.22:1, 0.91:1, 0.70:1; reverse 3.00:1

Four-speed automatic gearbox:
   (Honda type EAT)
   Ratios 2.65:1, 1.46:1, 0.97:1, 0.68:1; reverse 1.90:1

Axle ratio
4.20:1   All models

Suspension, steering and brakes
Front suspension with unequal length double
   wishbones, steel coil springs and elastomeric
   compound spring aids, co-axial telescopic dampers
   and anti-roll bar
Rear suspension with independent struts, transverse
   and trailing links, steel coil springs and elastomeric
   compound spring aids, telescopic dampers and anti-
   roll bar. Twin-wishbone rear suspension from 1988
   model year. Boge Nivomat self-levelling dampers
Honda speed proportional rack-and-pinion steering
   with power assistance as standard
Disc brakes all round, with single-cylinder floating
   calipers; handbrake acting on rear discs
Ventilated front discs with 285mm diameter. [Legend
   brakes smaller than 800]
Solid rear discs with 260mm diameter
Two diagonally split hydraulic circuits; ABS optional on
   early models and standard from 1988 model year

Dimensions

Overall length	189.4in (4,811mm) – saloon, 1986–88 model years
	190.6in (4,841mm) – saloon, 1989–90 model years
	184.6in (4,689mm) – saloon Japan
	188in (4,775) mm – coupé
Overall width	68.3in (1,735mm) – saloon 1986–88
	68.9in (1,750mm) – saloon 1989–90
	66.7in (1,694mm) – saloon Japan
	68.7in (1,745mm) – coupé
Overall height	54.7in (1,389mm) – saloon
	53.9in (1,369mm) – coupé
Wheelbase	108.7in (2,761mm) – saloon
	106.5in (2,705mm) – coupé
Front track	59in (1,500mm) – coupé
Rear track	59in (1,500mm) – coupé

Wheels and tyres
6J x 15 steel or alloy wheels with 205/60 VR 15 tyres

INDEX